MW01483982

EMOTIONAL

DEPENDENCY

ESSENTIAL STEPS IN OVERCOMING

EMOTIONAL DEPENDENCY

BY:

ESTER NOVAK

Table of Contents

INTRODUCTION

Emotional dependency is a personality disorder in which a person with low self-worth is constantly seeking security in other people, or in external factors, without trusting in his or her own interior criteria and resources.

Emotional dependency starts when a child is not loved appropriately by the people who mean the most to him, such parents, siblings, or other close people. This lack of love generates low self-esteem, a problem that tends to grow during adolescence. As an adult, the emotional dependent recreates situations where he plays a submissive role, always trying to please others in order to maintain the relationship bond at all costs, and thus avoid the terrifying prospect of rejection.

The lack of self-esteem from childhood on is the main cause of emotional dependency. It is the result of an emotional blackmail that teaches the child that she will be loved only after meeting the expectations of her parents or other meaningful people. Any effort to affirm herself or show her individuality will be reproved or punished. Her wings are cut, and she quickly learns not to create conflict or not to bother her parents if she wants to get the affection she needs.

Manipulation and feelings of guilt

Provoking guilt is a way to manipulate the child into having the "right" attitude. Mothers are often heard complaining about the way their children or husbands disappoint or annoy them; authoritarian fathers can often be heard saying in a disproportionate tone: "Be quiet, and do what I say" or "In this house you do what I tell you to do."

Failures in the construction of self-esteem

The child's self-esteem, and his capacity to be alone, is built through the reflection, or the mirror, of the trust his parents place in him. A child may have failures during this stage because his parents give him conflicting messages about his capacities; he is unable to interiorize those qualities and needs an adult by his side to feel secure.

Episodes of passion, indifference, abuse, and manipulation are manifestations of disordered, or even pathological, psychological patterns.

As humans, we tend to look for and reproduce what is familiar to us, what we've seen from our earliest childhood. These are behavioral patterns learned in childhood that leave a deep imprint on each human being.

So, it is a big mistake to confuse love with dependency and toxic relationships. This can happen, particularly, when a person's self-esteem is low, and they are looking for acceptance and love from others, even if it means compromising their own dignity.

The emotionally dependent accept scorn and abuse as something normal; they tend to feel attracted to people who seem to be very secure in themselves, and who have a dominant personality. Unfortunately, the emotionally dependent do not know genuine love between two people who respect each other and exchange affection; they have difficulty taking over the reins of their own lives and they hope to be "found" someday by that special person who will make them happy and end their solitude and existential anguish.

Some behaviors are clear indicators of unhealthy relationships, and they can gradually shift into a dangerous dependency, such as possession, manipulation, lack of respect, jealousy, insecurity, and abuse. These are symptoms of a fear of not being loved and accepted as we are. That's why people fall into situations of domination and submission — they try to ensure an apparent stability with a false affection and attention that can be transformed into a dependency, a "drug."

The secret is to build a couples relationship by developing the best part of ourselves and by choosing people who are compatible, and who also seek to bring out the best of themselves in respect, sincere esteem, attention, understanding, acceptance, and true affection.

The right environment is one that favors a love of self-giving, openness, and respect for the other person.

Knowing how to love and esteem ourselves is a healthy basis for being able to love and esteem the other, and to begin the search for a healthy and loving partner.

Some symptoms of emotional dependency:

- Constant and obsessive need to be close to other people

- Constant insecurity about the future
- Feeling of not being good enough to be with the other person
- Obsessive fear of losing love
- Constant feeling of guilt if they don't pay total attention to their partner
- Acceptance of psychological and physical suffering, for fear of losing the relationship
- A constant and dominant feeling of anxiety

CHAPTER 1

WHAT IS EMOTIONAL DEPENDENCY?

Love can be exhilarating, especially at the very beginning of a relationship. Everything you experience with your partner feels so new and overall amazing, and you think how nothing can go wrong.

Well some things can go wrong, including complete emotional dependency on your significant other.

Definition

Emotional dependency is when a woman allows others (like a significant other) to affect her feelings and emotions, and depends on them for happiness, etc. This is giving complete control to others over a woman's own emotions. This is unhealthy and can negatively impact self-esteem, since self-esteem is dependent on others. This is different from having a balanced relationship, where two people have interdependence and allow other to affect them only slightly emotionally. According to one relationship site, it is impossible to love others and not give them some control, but there needs to be a balance. Complete independence does not allow people to form connections with others.

Co-dependency as a broad definition is "dependence on the needs of or control by another," according to Merriam-

Webster. However, in the psychological sense, it is "a psychological condition or a relationship in which a person is controlled or manipulated by another who is affected with a pathological condition."

One study stated that "seven million American women are depressed, and 40 million Americans, primarily women, have been labeled as codependent."

Emotional dependency can also be found in people with dependent personality disorder, "a long-term (chronic) condition in which people depend too much on others to meet their emotional and physical needs," according to MedlinePlus, a service of the National Institutes of Health.

Understanding dependency

Mary Lamia, a clinical psychologist and psychoanalyst in California, said in an e-mail that she has dealt with women who are dependent in relationships.

"I've seen very accomplished [women] behaving in a dependent way in their partnerships because they grew up believing they had to give a depressed or narcissistic parent a sense of purpose by "needing" them," Lamia said.

There are also women who try to be independent but still have problems.

"I've also seen women in treatment who appear very independent in their partnerships, but they have an underlying fear that they will be abandoned if they express their needs," Lamia said.

This Article Self-esteem, which includes recognizing your value, and a "healthy sense of agency," which is "the ability to take action, influence your own life and assume responsibility for your actions," are important for health, she said.

"Optimal self-esteem and a strong sense of agency protect you and contribute to your stability as a separate person," Latmia said.

She said there has to be a balance between independence and dependence.

"When a woman over values herself and her self-esteem is at the extreme high level, this constitutes narcissism," Latmia said. "Sometimes it is healthy to be 'dependent' and have the ability to rely on another person. Being emotionally independent - at an optimal level - might imply that one's self-esteem is not based solely on the recognition by, and opinions of, one's partner."

Sudeepta Varma, a psychiatrist, said in a voicemail that emotionally dependency isn't a disorder and it isn't always present with a disorder, but some people with mental conditions like depression, anxiety and personality disorders can exhibit emotional dependency.

"If you're emotionally dependent to the extent that you can't make decisions or that it's affecting your life because of it or that you're making bad decisions because of it, then I would say that it's a problem," Varma said.

She said one way to be more emotionally independent is to "take control and start planning and scheduling their lives not around their partners or other people." People can also recognize their emotional needs and spread them out so they aren't only depending on one person. This includes having a variety of friends and even a therapist.

Women should also be able to accept their decisions and realize they did the best with what they had.

"Of course what we want to strive for is something called interdependence, where not only are you depending on other people, but you're also reliable and you can be there for them," Varma said. "You don't want to be there for [other] people at the expense of your own needs."

To summarize, here are the top five ways to become more emotionally independent in relationships and life from experts and from my own personal observations:

1. Recognize your self-worth and work on improving your self-esteem, which can be through focusing on positive thoughts about yourself, realizing your limitations and your achievements, working on goals, helping others and doing what makes you feel better. Accept your decisions and realize you are capable of doing what's best for yourself (and get help if you're not capable).

2. Realize that you control yourself, including your feelings, emotions and actions. Sometimes there are uncontrollable events in life, but you need to realize what you can control. Don't let someone else determine how your life will turn out.

3. Spread out and recognize your emotional needs and don't depend on one person. Work on building a

variety of friendships and even talk to a therapist or psychologist.

4. Don't schedule your life around everyone else. Realize that your needs are important and that you need to take control of your life and be independent. You can compromise and recognize others' needs, but remember that you have to live with yourself and you don't want to be miserable.

5. Awareness of all the above issues and about emotional dependency and co-dependency in general can allow you to work toward more independence and healthy relationships.

CHAPTER 2

EMOTIONAL DEPENDENCE AND CODEPENDENCY

Emotional dependence is a reluctance or refusal to emotionally accept the adult role. It is like being a child, in that other people ('the real adults') are expected to 'make things right.' At the same time, adult freedom and autonomy is insisted upon. This mismatch leads to great complication in trying to form loving, or cooperative adult relationships. The most prominent behaviors are based in refusing to take responsibility for:

- Ones emotions
- Ones situation
- The results of one's decisions

Traits Indicating Emotional Dependence:

- Requests for reassurance
- 'Addictive relationships'
- Blaming
- Avoiding making major decisions
- Complaints of insolvable problems
- Inability/unwillingness to make decisions
- Procrastination

- Getting one or more people to intervene in natural consequences through sympathy or codependency
- Low self-esteem
- Disguised infantile grandiosity
- Feel that what they like to do anyway should be rewarded with a living.
- Rebellion, passive aggression, and inability to cooperate.
- Inability to either commit to something or decline it.
- Asking frequently for advice, but not following it or finding fault with it.

Emotionally dependent people often acquire a great deal of knowledge or skill, but have trouble sustaining a career or position in which the knowledge and skill is reliably implemented. Often they have lofty pursuits that are never pursued realistically or tested. From the position of dependence, it is possible to appear brilliant, innovative, talented, because topics and subjects can be mentally and verbally pursued without the constraint of arranging and executing practical steps. Often courses of study or expertise are launched very eagerly, but abandoned before completion, or the educational part is completed but the vocational part is not sustained.

Emotionally dependent people may create a role in a family or group in which they seem to point the way forward, but others actually are often doing the day to day work and deciding daily practical matters. Such pseudo-leadership flounders eventually, however, often only after the period of enthusiasm is over.

Frequently, however, emotionally dependent people are in a position of 'collapse,' 'not doing very well,' or in a crisis. and are being helped, rescued, or tended to by others. From this position they do not get on their feet easily because typical human struggles and social friction are experienced as trauma or setbacks. One illusory way out of collapse is an addictive relationship, described in the latter part of this webpage.

The Advice Bind:

A fundamental and frequent transaction for an emotionally dependent person is to ask another adult or teen for advice about what to do. Whatever advice is received is neither clearly rejected nor accepted, but rather whatever downsides exist are exhaustively recited. All choices have some downside that is the nature of a decision. An emotionally dependent person is very reluctant to accept a downside, and certainly unwilling to accept responsibility for a downside. This puts enormous burden on the advice giver to present options as if they had no downside (which contains a dishonesty that the emotionally dependent person will usually point out!) There can be a feeling that the emotionally dependent person just wants the situation fixed by someone else, but this fix requires retention of upsides and protection from downsides. Conversations about the issue can be very frequent, or very long, with no obvious way to fulfill or complete the advising role. A feeling of helplessness will pervade. This, if anything, is the gist of the phrase, "being clingy" or "being needy." Most people are glad to help someone, but are frustrated when asked for help but unable to either help or end the interaction.

Asymmetrical Relationships

Emotional dependence is most often 'self-treated' through relationships. Emotionally dependent people tend always to be in a relationship. They tend to hang on to relationships as long as possible, but will usually start another relationship quickly if the existing one does end. At the very early stages of a new relationship, an emotionally dependent person will put his or her least dependent behavior forward. This is not nefarious or even conscious-- all people tend to behave in the way they sense is desirable in the early stages of a relationship.

But once some commitment occurs, emotionally dependent adults tend to decompensate functionally over time, and the non-dependent partner is drawn into becoming an enabler. This dynamic is never really stable unless there are children or external forces holding it together. In a relationship with two emotionally dependent partners, however, there will be great stability but also great strife and conflict. This gives rise to the term addictive relationships, which is described below.

Mutually Dependent (or 'Addictive') Relationships

Emotional dependence can divide into two subtypes: counterdependent and codependent. Relationships formed from one member of each group will intensify the respective tendencies and tend to be especially strife filled but extremely difficult to end. This is because of four main interlocking trait polarities listed below:

Counter-dependent	Co-dependent
Grandiosity	Insecurity
Independence	Dependence
Self-Centeredness	Other-Centeredness
Intrusiveness	Lack of Boundaries

Counter-dependents include 'rage-oholics', sociopaths, most addicts, and all narcissists. Some native codependents can function as counter-dependents through being addicted. The 'sick role' of having many medical issues can also be a place for a counter-dependent. Counter-dependents appear superficially secure but 'secretly' feel insecure and fearful. Instead of real assertiveness there is a blind demandingness and entitlement. Counter-dependents exhibit all the behavior listed in the bulleted lists above in the top section, but they disguise it with bluster or verbal attacks. Codependents, on the other hand, are openly insecure but secretly feel controlling.

Both these subtypes may disguise the 'dependent' picture described in the top sections of this page. But make no mistake, both types are emotionally dependent in that they do not take responsibility for situations and results, rather they place that on the partner, or third persons.

Each of the four main polarities are discussed in greater detail below.

Counter-dependent	Co-dependent
Powerful	Ineffectual
Self-confident	Uncertain

Self-important	Insignificant
Entitled	Deprived
Special or Unique	Unremarkable

Apart from rare episodes of collapse, counter-dependents are grandiose. They need a partner that will allow them to maintain their illusion of strength and power. Conversely codependents feel inadequate and "not enough". They seek strong partners who can make them feel complete and effective.

However, both grandiosity and undisguised insecurity are based on emotional dependence. There is a underlying belief that one cannot cope with life naturally. The counter-dependent strategy focuses on and exaggerates strengths while denying and blocking discussion of weaknesses. The codependent strategy focuses on and exaggerates weaknesses while blocking awareness of strengths. There is a tacit agreement: the codependent will not challenge the power of the counter-dependent, if the counter-dependent will not challenge the codependent's excuses of being ineffectual.

The codependent reenacts and maintains deprivation by serving the entitlement of the counter-dependent. The codependent may acknowledge the excessiveness of the demands (that is the point-- to be burdened or deprived) but he or she still complies and feels they have no other option. Codependents comply with the wishes of others even when they do not like what is asked or have doubts.

Counter-dependents feel confident. This is a positive trait if yoked with realism and tested in the world. Taken to extremes, self-confidence leads to schemes involving control and manipulation that fall apart and leave consequences for other to clean up (without getting the credit.) Counter-dependents are often very appealing because they will promise great things, tell others what they want to hear, think big, and engender enthusiasm in others. The counter-dependent does not see this as insincere because getting what is wanted is seen as the ultimate truth.

Codependents love the grandiose traits of the counter-dependent because they want to be supplied from the outside with the certainty that they lack. They look for an emotional leader to help light up their desire. In the beginning at least the codependent admires the counter-dependent. Later they may become the counter-dependents greatest critic but the thing that remains the same is that they let the counter-dependent set the agenda, and they almost always comply in some way with the demands.

Counter-dependents need constant reinforcement and reassurance and codependents supply this instinctively but may also learn to feed the counter-dependents ego deliberately to manage his or her mood and keep peace.

Co-dependents' insecurity drives a compulsion to fix or take care of others. This makes them vulnerable to exploitation. But there is always an edge of controllingness to this help. Conspicuously, however, codependents are unable or unwilling to work hard for themselves. They believe that they really cannot be successful so the best they can hope is to make success available for someone else.

Codependents meet others needs without being asked, and this dovetails with counter-dependents who are needy but do not like to admit having needs. Codependents consistently give more than they receive and believe this is noble. They do the thinking for others but do not take the credit. They frequently suffer the consequences of others actions.

Codependents set very low goals for themselves and fail to hone their non-caretaking abilities. They constantly put themselves down and have trouble taking compliments. They live in emotional deprivation. Being with someone that feels terrible about themselves makes counter-dependents feel powerful by contrast. Codependents repeatedly come to the counter-dependent for encouragement and advice, despite a history of receiving discouragement and direction that has led to trouble.

Codependents have fantasies of being the perfect helper or a stoic victim (as in sacrifice), which is an inverted type of grandiosity. Codependents will also show a certain grandiosity and stubbornness if confronted and asked to take responsibility for their traits--this is a shared aspect of emotional dependence.

1. Independent------------Dependent

Counter-dependent	**Co-dependent**
Trust Self	Trust Others
Distrust Others	Distrust Self

Over-identify with Strengths	Over-identify with Weaknesses
Deny Weaknesses	Deny Strengths
Demanding	Complying
Praise Seeking	Approval Seeking

Counterdependents seek partners who, whatever they hope for, do not insist on a emotional connection or real intimacy, because counterdependents are oriented to a sexual or practical exchange. It is possible for counterdependents not to be in an official relationship but just use all their tactics to draw out the codependent behavior of neighbors, co-workers, helping professionals, and even strangers.

Counterdependents appear extremely independent. They trust their own abilities and when something goes wrong they attempt to fix it themselves. However, if the fix isn't quick or easy, they will manipulate someone else, usually a codependent, into taking care of it, usually by blaming or sulking. Counterdependents identify with strengths and build not only their identity but their daily routines around them. That is why counterdependents live unbalanced lifestyles where many basic areas are neglected. They also devalue anything they are not good at. Counterdependents are constantly acting like they are proving themselves and are frequently competitive over trivial matters.

Counterdependents have high expectations of others and demand things without hesitation. They are often disappointed (because of unrealistic expectations) and they will use this real if manufactured disappointment as a justification for their entitlement.

Counterdependents seek praise and recognition from others. If they do not get the 'correct' response from their partner they will seek it from others. If they receive criticism they respond with rage, shame, and humiliation (which they attempt to hide). Codependents find it meaningful that they detect the weakness which the counterdependent attempts to hide.

Codependents have an exaggerated sense of the importance and abilities of others. They may trust others even when it is irrational to do so. In fact codependents are usually very competent in in practical maters. This is demonstrated by one, how smoothly they take care of themselves when the counterdependent is 'out of action' (in jail, in hospital, on a spree, pursuing a scheme) and by two, how they take care of unglamorous details on a daily basis for the counterdependent. Despite this codependents are known for professing incompetence. Codependents use the vehemence of the counterdependent to substitute for their will, which fits into the reluctance of an emotionally dependent person to take responsibility for decisions (but within this context, codependents make many smaller decisions on how to implement what is demanded from them).

Codependents seek approval. Because of this they are constantly coerced by the possibility or actuality of disapproval. They share with counterdependents the felt need to be perfect, but unlike the counterdependent they feel they will always be insignificant.

Codependents are in fact very good helpers--they do tasks no one else wants to. If criticized, they usually assume it is accurate. They will try harder at a task even if it is unsatisfying or impossible.

2. Self Centered------------Other Centered

Counterdependent	Codependent
Insensitive	Oversensitive
Selfish	Altruistic
Exploitative	Nurturing

A counterdependent does not worry about the codependent leaving. If this happens, which is rare, the counterdependent usually quickly finds someone who will cater to his or her needs. The codependent constantly worries about the counter-dependent leaving. However neither party hardly ever actually leaves, threats aside.

Counterdependents demand attention. They depersonalize others and make them into objects. Counterdependents don't know what other people are thinking and feeling and typically don't care because they are pre-occupied with their own needs. To recognize the feelings of others would require recognizing their own feelings which is avoided strenuously. Counterdependents are skillful with dealing with things, they have trouble dealing with real people who have feelings and values. Counterdependents manipulate and bully others to achieve their own ends, styling this behavior as obtaining justice or "what is right."

Codependents have an excessive tolerance for inappropriate, annoying, or inconveniencing behavior. They are oversensitive to the needs of others and will do anything to make others comfortable. Codependents are preoccupied with the needs of other and this distracts them from personal problems or introspection. They tend to comply with demands automatically and are attracted to demanding people. When asked what they want or what they feel, codependents frequently reply with a narrative of the actions of their counterdependent.

Codependents are comfortable with self-centered people because they don't expect empathy, attention, or caring. They find it acceptable to be ignored and have their needs ignored. They hope for a reversal of this in the future (which never comes). Counterdependents are uncomfortable with any discussion about unmet needs or wants because they feel their presence and actions should already be ensuring the satisfaction of those around them. Codependents, on their part dislike putting forth their needs, so the combination usually ensures that the codependent's needs and wants never get discussed. Codependents can only relate by giving something, counterdependents can only relate by getting something. Of course both can conceptualize an exchange but neither can conceptualize mutual satisfaction, for different reasons.

Codependents are over-sensitive to the needs of others and will do anything to make others comfortable.

Codependents sacrifice for others but have difficulty accumulating things for themselves, including simple comforts and common conveniences. Codependents will feel gratitude for scraps or small tokens. Codependent readily share but also confuse sharing with giving everything away. They protect themselves by giving others what they want.

3. Intrusive---------------Receptive

Counterdependent	Codependent
Rigid Boundaries	Lack of Boundaries
Well Defended	Poorly Defended
Aggressive	Passive
Intrusiveness	Lack of Boundaries

Counterdependents frequently invade the the privacy of others without a thought. They think they are entitled to be as close as they want, but also free to break it off when they want. Counterdependents have rigid psychological boundaries that keep others at a distance. It's not possible to get close to them unless they want one to. Counterdependents are well-defended, meaning the opinions of others do not hurt or affect them (unless they are criticized directly) Counterdependents go after what they want aggressively. They treat life as a battleground

Codependents lack boundaries. They allow others to invade their privacy and perhaps believe even their thoughts cannot be kept private. They are used to merging with others but always feel abandoned when the other breaks it off. Even when they set the boundary (because of an extreme situation)

they feel abandoned. Codependents let others get real close real fast. Codependents are not well-defended, when others express displeasure the codependent tends to conform or comply or feel great guilt.

Codependents are passive when it comes to getting things in the world against resistance. They often attempt to get things by overwork and excessive contribution but this is not real aggression. Codependents hope that the aggressiveness of the counterdependent will serve them eventually, and they may act quite aggressively or even 'out of character' at the counterdependent's behest and urging, perhaps even doing the 'dirty work' or seducing others.

Counterdependents are always setting the agenda (sometimes called 'defining reality'), and codependents may argue or resist (ineffectively) but always within that agenda. Counterdependents frequently will speak for the codependent, who will not only allow it, but may even feel relief.

Counterdependents often have cyclical behavior, basically alternating periods of civil behavior (during which tension slowly rises) with periods of acting-out, dominating, and abusive behavior (during which tension is released). Codependents often fail to recognize the cyclical nature, responding repeatedly to the civil periods with hope and plans ("we've finally turned a corner") and responding to abusive periods with crisis management and enabling ("we just need to get through this")

The only feelings counterdependents are interested in are excitement, passion, and intensity. All other feelings hurt and are avoided. Those people or events that trigger other feelings are attacked. Secretly codependents crave excitement and passion too, but cannot seek them directly and are hoping to be lead there by the counterdependent. This communicates to others that their job is 'turn on' the counterdependent. For both codependent and counterdependent, there is an inability to experience real pleasure, the sharing of which is the basis for true love. The relationship becomes a refuge from the world with increasing isolation from other people.

Symptoms of Codependency

Codependency is characterized by a person belonging to a dysfunctional, one-sided relationship where one person relies on the other for meeting nearly all of their emotional and self-esteem needs. It also describes a relationship that enables another person to maintain their irresponsible, addictive, or underachieving behavior.

Do you expend all of your energy in meeting your partner's needs? Do you feel trapped in your relationship? Are you the one that is constantly making sacrifices in your relationship?

The term codependency has been around for decades. Although it originally applied to spouses of alcoholics (first called co-alcoholics), researchers revealed that the characteristics of codependents were much more prevalent in the general population than had previously imagined. In fact, they found that if you were raised in a dysfunctional family or had an ill parent, you could also be codependent.

Researchers also found that codependent symptoms got worse if left untreated. The good news is that they're reversible.

Symptoms of Codependency

The following is a list of symptoms of codependency and being in a codependent relationship. You don't need to have them all to qualify as codependent.

- *Low self-esteem.*Feeling that you're not good enough or comparing yourself to others are signs of low self-esteem. The tricky thing about self-esteem is that some people think highly of themselves, but it's only a disguise — they actually feel unlovable or inadequate. Underneath, usually hidden from consciousness, are feelings of shame.Guilt and perfectionism often go along with low self-esteem. If everything is perfect, you don't feel bad about yourself.

- *People-pleasing.*It's fine to want to please someone you care about, but codependents usually don't think they have a choice. Saying "No" causes them anxiety. Some codependents have a hard time saying "No" to anyone. They go out of their way and sacrifice their own needs to accommodate other people.

- *Poor boundaries.*Boundaries are sort of an imaginary line between you and others. It divides up what's yours and somebody else's, and that applies not only to your body, money, and belongings, but also to your feelings, thoughts and needs. That's especially where codependents get into trouble. They have blurry or weak boundaries. They feel responsible for other people's feelings and problems or blame their own on someone else.Some codependents have rigid boundaries. They are closed off and withdrawn, making it hard for other people to get close to them. Sometimes, people flip back and forth between having weak boundaries and having rigid ones.

- *Reactivity.*A consequence of poor boundaries is that you react to everyone's thoughts and feelings. If someone says something you disagree with, you either believe it or become defensive. You absorb their words, because there's no boundary. With a boundary, you'd realize it was just their opinion and not a reflection of you and not feel threatened by disagreements.

- *Caretaking.*Another effect of poor boundaries is that if someone else has a problem, you want to help them to the point that you give up yourself. It's natural to feel empathy and sympathy for someone, but codependents start putting other people ahead of themselves. In fact, they need to help and might feel rejected if another person doesn't want help. Moreover, they keep trying to help and fix the other person, even when that person clearly isn't taking their advice.

- *Control.*Control helps codependents feel safe and secure. Everyone needs some control over events in their life. You wouldn't want to live in constant uncertainty and chaos, but for codependents, control limits their ability to take risks and share their feelings. Sometimes they have an addiction that either helps them loosen up, like alcoholism, or helps them hold their feelings down, like workaholism, so that they don't feel out of control.Codependents also need to control those close to them, because they need other people to behave in a certain way to feel okay. In fact, people-pleasing and care-taking can be used to control and manipulate people. Alternatively, codependents are bossy and tell you what you should or shouldn't do. This is a violation of someone else's boundary.

- *Dysfunctional communication.*Codependents have trouble when it comes to communicating their thoughts, feelings and needs. Of course, if you don't know what you think, feel or need, this becomes a problem. Other times, you know, but you won't own up to your truth. You're afraid to be truthful, because you don't want to upset someone else. Instead of saying, "I don't like that," you might pretend that it's okay or tell someone what to do. Communication becomes dishonest and confusing when you try to manipulate the other person out of fear.

- *Obsessions.*Codependents have a tendency to spend their time thinking about other people or relationships. This is caused by their dependency and anxieties and fears. They can also become obsessed when they think they've made or might make a "mistake."Sometimes you can lapse into fantasy about how you'd like things to be or about someone you love as a way to avoid the pain of the present. This is one way to stay in denial, discussed below, but it keeps you from living your life.

- *Dependency.*Codependents need other people to like them to feel okay about themselves. They're afraid of being rejected or abandoned, even if they can function on their own. Others need always to be in a relationship, because they feel depressed or lonely when they're by themselves for too long. This trait makes it hard for them to end a relationship, even when the relationship is painful or abusive. They end up feeling trapped.

- *Denial.* One of the problems people face in getting help for codependency is that they're in denial about it, meaning that they don't face their problem. Usually they think the problem is someone else or the situation. They either keep complaining or trying to fix the other person, or go from one relationship or job to another and never own up the fact that they have a problem.Codependents also deny their feelings and needs. Often, they don't know what they're feeling and are instead focused on what others are feeling. The same thing goes for their needs. They pay attention to other people's needs and not their own. They might be in denial of their need for space and autonomy. Although some codependents seem needy, others act like they're self-sufficient when it comes to needing help. They won't reach out and have trouble receiving. They are in denial of their vulnerability and need for love and intimacy.

- *Problems with intimacy.* By this I'm not referring to sex, although sexual dysfunction often is a reflection of an intimacy problem. I'm talking about being open and close with someone in an intimate relationship. Because of the shame and weak boundaries, you might fear that you'll be judged, rejected, or left. On the other hand, you may fear being smothered in a relationship and losing your autonomy. You might deny your need for closeness and feel that your partner wants too much of your time; your partner complains that you're unavailable, but he or she is denying his or her need for separateness.

- *Painful emotions.* Codependency creates stress and leads to painful emotions. Shame and low self-esteem create anxiety and fear about being judged, rejected or abandoned; making mistakes; being a failure; feeling trapped by being close or being alone. The other symptoms lead to feelings of anger and resentment, depression, hopelessness, and despair. When the feelings are too much, you can feel numb.

There is help for recovery and change for people who are codependent. The first step is getting guidance and support. These symptoms are deeply ingrained habits and difficult to identify and change on your own. Join a 12-Step program, such as Codependents Anonymous or seek counseling. Work on becoming more assertive and building your self-esteem.

CHAPTER 3

TYPES OF EMOTIONAL DEPENDENCE

Emotional dependence is a complex condition. Generally it does not obey any one rule, and creating it and maintaining it are two different things. In many cases, it's also not even a conscious reality. On the contrary, the person with emotional dependence thinks that the problems derived from their dependence have a different, and often external, origin.

Behind the dependence, there is usually extreme fear. There are also many fantasies about one's own ability or place in the world. One feels, without evidence to support it, that if he broke or lacked certain bonds, he would be in grave danger.

This type of dependency is similar to that experienced by an addict. As such, it also entails an abstention syndrome. Episodes of anxiety and depression appear when, for some reason, the bond breaks or weakens momentarily. Existence itself can feel unbearable without that bond. Whoever suffers from it undoubtedly suffers greatly. Three basic types of emotional dependence can be discussed and are as follows.

Emotional Dependence of the Family

This is one of the most difficult forms of emotional dependence to overcome. It usually corresponds to family structures where the parents suffer strong states of anxiety and transmit it to their children. The latter are educated with excessive fear of the world. Anything external is seen as a threat and the family is seen as a shelter.

hose who suffer from this type of dependence overestimate the protection offered by the family. While there are often affectionate bonds and great gestures of solidarity, it is also true that there are insane traits, including the repeated idea that there is risk and the further we are from it, the better.

In these types of families, self-confidence is not encouraged. On the contrary, the bottom line is the belief that the person will be incapable of facing big challenges. In this way, the family becomes a kind of bubble that shelters but also incarcerates. This is the wrong way to deal with anxiety. It is also a vague response to the need to grow and be autonomous.

Emotional Dependence of the Couple

This type of dependency is one of the most frequent. It is also one of the most harmful. It is part of an erroneous belief that assumes the couple gives meaning to their own life or protects them from terrible loneliness. That is why the couple becomes the axis of life itself.

This type of dependency is typical of people who carry great insecurities. They are not clear about what they are or are not capable of doing. In fact, they assume they are very helpless. Therefore, they need support to live and that kind of support comes from their partner. This becomes a kind of protective shield against suffering or fear. That is why a strong attachment develops.

Although this type of dependence can work for a while, the truth is that sooner or later it causes great suffering. The dependent person is so afraid of losing their partner that they can develop very harmful behavior, including excessive jealousy or unlimited submission. Thus, dependence deteriorates the relationship rather than making it stronger.

Emotional dependence on the social environment

The most characteristic aspect of this condition is an excessive need to be recognized and approved of in any environment. If there are not sufficient signs of true appreciation and acceptance, the individual panics. In addition, he will do whatever is necessary to achieve that apparent psychological compensation. Feeling rejected, from their perspective, is the worst thing that could ever happen to them.

To achieve approval, one may become servile or invisible. In the first place, the dependent person feels compelled to please others, even overexerting themselves. They will make any sacrifice so they don't have to face rejection or confrontation. In the second case, the person relinquishes their convictions in order to dissipate tension in the environment. In both cases, the situation is completely damaging.

In the case of family dependence, couple dependence and dependence on the social environment, what lies deep within is poor self-esteem. Above all, there is no awareness of what one is capable of doing. It starts from the idea that one has little value and is not able to get through life without others.

All those false beliefs translate into fear and anxiety. And as with all unjustified fears that we hold, the best way to overcome it is to face it. Maybe you just need to take your first step. Dare to walk alone. Risk getting out of your comfort zone. Self-confidence is not built overnight, but one thing is certain: if you build it away from your "dependencies," it will be much more solid.

DIFFERENCES BETWEEN BEING EMOTIONALLY DEPENDENT AND ACTUALLY IN LOVE

1. You are actually happy when you spend time together. This seems obvious, but when you're really in love with someone, you like being with them. When you're emotionally dependent on them, you don't actually enjoy most of the time you spend together, but still feel as though you should stick it out because you're "meant" to be with this person.

2. You can be happy when you aren't together. On the flip side, if you're really in love with someone you can likewise love spending time alone and see it as a healthy part of your relationship. If you're emotionally dependent, spending time alone is scary and try to avoid it at all costs.

3. What freaks you out about potentially breaking up with them is the idea of not having them in your life, not "being alone" or "being single until

age X." What you fear when you think about losing someone can tell you a lot about how you really feel about them. If what hurts the most about a potential breakup is the idea that you would have to "start over" or sleep alone or be financially on your own as opposed to, you know, lose someone you love, you're probably more dependent on them than you think.

4. You're engaging with life more, as opposed to withdrawing from it because you're in a relationship. Love opens you up. Dependency (fear) closes you, and leads you to isolate yourself with your partner more and more.

5. You don't have a deep fear of losing their approval. You don't have to qualify your opinions before you share them, you can speak freely, aren't shy about your tastes in music or books, and wear the clothes that you like. They make you want to be more of yourself, not less.

6. Your partner is not playing mind games with you, refusing to commit or continually hurting you. Your love is healthy. The most obvious difference between love and dependency is simply the quality of your relationship: this person treats you with all the love and respect you give them in return.

7. You never feel pressured into doing something that your partner wants and you don't. Whether it's sexual or social or anything else, you never

feel like you have to pretend you want to do something you don't in order to stay in your partner's good graces. Your comfort is ultimately more important to them than temporary desires.

8.   You began your relationship from a place of love, not a place of desperation. You got together because you were falling in love, not because you were reaching a certain age and they were the most decent person to come along, or because you could barely function emotionally when you were on your own and needed someone to take care of you.

9.   Your relationship brings you more peace, comfort and bliss than it ever does fear, jealousy or worry. It's completely normal to feel jealous once in a while, or worry about something going wrong, but when you're really in the right relationship, the positive exponentially outweighs it all. When you're in a relationship in which you're emotionally dependent, there's far more "fear of loss" than there is anything else.

10.   You love your partner for who they are, not how much they love you. When you think of why you care about your partner and want to spend so much of your life with them, it's because of their personality traits, how kind they are, how much they make you laugh or think or feel at ease. You love them, not just the fact that they love you.

KEYS TO OVERCOMING EMOTIONAL DEPENDENCE

We human beings are "social animals" and we need others; that is indisputable. But how much do we need them? Where is the line that distinguishes a healthy connection from an emotional addiction?

Contact with others is necessary for our development. Children need someone to care for them, someone who not only gives them food, but also human warmth and affection. In order to have a fulfilled life when we grow up, it is necessary for us to have a social circle: relatives, friends, a partner…

But it is one thing to talk about the need for social contact in general, and another altogether to discuss concrete relationships that we dedicate ourselves to and to how we live them.

Emotional dependence

Often, and especially in partner relationships, emotional dependency or addiction comes into play, and the relationship, far from being a form of support, turns into an obstacle for

the development and even for the mental health of the two partners.

If you are not happy in your relationship, it could possibly be due to the fact that you are living in a position of addiction. As such, we are going to describe for you some of the signs that may indicate some level of emotional addiction to your partner.

1. In the first place, if your relationship brings you suffering (such as sadness or anxiety) and you still feel incapable of changing paths or leaving them, it is highly probable that you have some degree of emotional dependence. Relationships are complicated and require effort, but not suffering.

2. One of the most concrete signs of addiction is that you are not doing any activity outside of the relationship. Be it a hobby, studies, a career, friends... if everything you do is with your partner, your relationship is probably addictive or dependent.

3. Another characteristic of an addiction to your partner is the inability to be alone. Maybe you have gotten so used to sharing everything with your partner that you no longer know what to do when you are alone, or maybe it is also possible that worry overwhelms you: worry that something could happen to them or about what they could be doing.

4. You have thoughts or you believe that you could not live without that person or that our life would have no meaning without them, that they are your whole world. These ideas are characteristic of a dependent relationship.

5. Jealousy is often another good indicator of an addictive relationship, as it is related to insecurity and a lack of communication.

Emotional dependence can have many causes. In some cases, it may be due to the fact that we have not learned to tolerate the suffering inherent in life and therefore we are not able to abandon partners that hurt us because we are afraid of change or being alone. In extreme cases, we may be unable to leave even if we're suffering mistreatment or abuse.

In other cases, because of self-esteem issues, we end up being dependent on our partners to make us feel good about ourselves, admire us, or give us the security that we do not have ourselves.

CHAPTER 4

HOW TO STOP EMOTIONAL DEPENDENCY

When we allow our happiness to rely too much on another person, it can have some dangerous consequences for our peace of mind and wellbeing. Emotional dependence is a real challenge and a real difficulty to overcome. It takes a great deal of courage to tap into the strengths that help us get beyond our need for others, but it's necessary in order for us to reach our true potential.

Having a certain amount of emotional dependency in our partners is normal, but when our happiness comes to rely on them, it becomes an unbalanced and unhealthy. It's vital for our partners to offer support when it's needed, but anything outside of that can be crippling.

Learning how stand on your own is painful, and it takes facing some uncomfortable truths and traumas that you might prefer to leave buried. Finding our presence and discovering the strength to stand on our own two feet is a beautiful thing, though, and something that's required for finding our way to true happiness.

How to tell if you've got an emotional dependence problem.

Often, we mistake our feelings of obsession or dependence for feelings of love or attraction. It's easy to lose yourself in those feelings and, if not properly identified, lose your authenticity in the process.

Dependence is not love and it never can be.

This idea starts as children, when we're not appropriately loved by the people who mean the most to us, and it's perpetuated over time as we jump from one loveless coupling to the next. When we miss out on this love as a child, we search for it constantly as an adult; the longing never goes away, it just stronger.

How the dependence wheels start turning.

Having such a lack of love leads to feelings of low self-esteem. This inability to value and trust ourselves creates a negative cycle of need which can feed the disorders that cause us to constantly seek security in others. It's the result of emotional blackmail that teaches us that in order to have worth, we have to meet impossible and even deplorable expectations. Over and over again, we out ourselves in a submissive role, hoping to reduce the years of damage that's been done.

It's not possible to be healed by someone else, though. You have to heal that broken child that lives inside you on your own.

That starts with recognizing when you have a problem with emotional dependence and it ends with taking the steps you need to correct this dependence and increase your confidence.

Recognizing the problem.

Emotionally dependent people aren't just insecure, they have an obsessive need to be close to and attached to other people. This kind of extreme insecurity also leads to insecurity about the future and an obsessive fear of losing love.

Dependent people have an almost-insane fear of not being good enough, which comes from their deep-rooted childhood traumas and disappointments. They also have a constant feeling of anxiety that makes it hard for them to accept the psychological and physical sufferings that come along with love and loss.

In the right environment, a dependent person can be giving, loving and compassionate to a fault, but trigger the fear and they turn into a different person entirely.

Living in this constant state of flux and fear is destructive to who we are at our core, but recognizing it takes patience. The secret to building relationships that last is not preventing the hurts of the past, it's developing the best parts of ourselves for the future, but coming to recognize that is difficult to do.

The dangers of emotional dependence.

For those of us with parents and grandparents from the bygone and Baby Boomer ages, we know first hand the dangers of emotional dependence.

Our mothers and grandmothers came from an age when dependence was the only means to survival for women. They were coached to base all of their happiness on the success and happiness of the people around them, rather than themselves, and this led to a whole host of problems later on down the road when they realized their lives had value.

Emotional dependence is dangerous and even more so when we fail to recognize it in time to prevent its nefarious patterns. Depending on others for our happiness is to build a castle on shifting sands. You're setting yourself up for failure and you're setting yourself up for danger.

A loss of self-esteem.

Though emotional dependence stems from a lack of self-esteem, it's also a self-esteem destroyer of its own, undermining our confidence subtly and over time.

When we become too dependent emotionally on our spouse or partner, we run the risk of losing the person that we love by losing ourselves. Our insecurities compact and compound, eating away at our confidence and our relationships as we lose touch with the person we were when the relationship began.

Isolation and loss of social skills.

Finding ourselves in such toxic, all-consuming relationships can cause us to isolate ourselves and lose touch with our friends. When we cut off our connection with the outside world, we quickly lose the social skills that are invaluable to our long-term happiness.

Feeling as though we are trapped and without strength leads us little by little to isolate ourselves more from the things and people that fill our lives with joy. It also encourages us to turn inward, stoking our inner critic and destroying our self-confidence over time.

Physical and psychological abuse.

Isolating ourselves with partners who we rely on for everything from our happiness to our sustenance amplifies the dangers and possibility of physical and psychological abuse in a relationship.

At some point, one partner may misunderstand the other partner's dependence to be a sign of weakness. This situation can lead to an imbalance of power and one partner assuming the "dominant role". The longer isolation occurs, the more sinister this dominant role can become, until one or both spouses find themselves in an especially dangerous and destructive situation.

It's not uncommon to find serious abuse in relationships where emotional dependency is high. When one person feels as though someone is entirely dependent on them for happiness, it becomes easier for them to act out by exerting pressure, lying, being hostile or even contemptuous.

Destruction of wellbeing.

Emotional dependency isn't just a state of mind. It's a verifiable psychological disorder that's manifested in many different ways and in many different stages of our lives.

Being dependent on another person runs deep, and being such a critical part of who we are it plays a big part where our emotions and wellbeing are concerned. Dependent people often suffer from "dysphoric moods" or sudden mood changes that make them unpredictable and difficult to deal with. They can also suffer from degraded mental states and often suffer with depression, stress, anxiety and severe feelings of guilt, emptiness and loneliness (despite their relationship status).

How To Stop Your Emotional Dependency.

Unfortunately, there's no hard-and-fast rulebook when it comes to dealing with emotional dependency. In many cases, getting past the traumas that manifest this disorder take professional help, but there are steps we can take to help get ourselves past our weakest moment.

Note: Emotional dependency is serious. If you think that you might be dealing with problematic dependence issues, reach out to someone you trust or a professional with experience in relevant traumas.

If emotional dependence is something you've been struggling with for a long tie, further your understanding by using these simple techniques for getting back in touch with the strong, authentic person you are inside.

1. Practice being there for yourself.

We all want to connect with other people, but it's our connection to self that has the most transformative powers. It's important to learn to look after yourself and it's important to learn that you can depend on you — no matter what.

Your needs won't go away just because you ignore them or just because someone else dismisses them. You are important and you deserved to be valued for who and what you are simply because you are a human being alive on this planet.

Practice being there for yourself by recognizing your needs and understanding that it is okay to prioritize them over the desires of others. Embrace your passions, interest and curiosities with open arms and don't hide yourself or your light be dampening it for someone else's glow.

We can learn to love ourselves but it takes a willing commitment, just like any other relationship. Sure, you may not be able to fulfil all your own needs, but you can fulfil most of them. You just have to roll up your sleeves and give it a try, instead of waiting on someone else to fulfil them for you.

Tips for being there for yourself more often: Recognize your needs and prioritize your wellbeing. Manage your needs regularly and don't be afraid to stick up for them. Treat yourself every week, but also do something for your future each week (like save). Do some regular physical exercise and refuse to let yourself wallow when you could be doing something productive.

2. Stop giving away your responsibilities to self.

When we aren't sure how to look after ourselves emotionally, it becomes convenient to pass the responsibility off to someone else, but that's a definitive way to find yourself in trouble. After all, no one can look after your emotions but you.

In order to become the strongest and most stable version of ourselves, we have to be able to develop our self-reliance.

This self-reliance makes us more resilient to the stress that life throws our way and makes it survivable when our loved ones let us down.

Giving away our responsibilities is weak and it encourages more weakness in our lives. Self-reliance is the key to escaping our needier and nastier traits, but it's a hard tool to master and an even harder one to maintain. Be kind to yourself and have the courage to stand up for the things you need most. No one is going to provide those things but you. The sooner you realize that, the better off you'll be.

3. **Re-parent yourself.**

If you're someone that came from a broken home or a broken family, learning how to lovingly re-parent yourself can be an invaluable tool to turning things around for the better.

It is often our broken inner child that is responsible for the heartbreaks of our adult lives.

These poorly and broken beings dwell within each of us, and have an uncanny way of rearing their heartbroken faces each time we face stress or adversity in our lives. Dealing with our inner children can be difficult, but it's necessary to cultivate healing in our lives.

Learning to tap into this inner child also allows you to lovingly reparent yourself, though, and that's a skill that's priceless. The art of re-parenting ourselves starts with sensing and genuinely expressing the hurts of injured inner child and ends with resolving them peacefully and rationally through understanding.

When we allow the child inside of us to be vulnerable, we allow ourselves to be as we are. Resolving to help this broken child with loving intention allows you to express yourself honestly and openly. Don't be afraid to let the little being know that their feelings are scary but harmless. Tell them that they will pass in time, but they have to be brave enough to let them go. You can follow this up with a statement of action, but whatever you do let the pain in and let yourself feel it and embrace it fully.

Develop a process with this child that allows you to handle your emotions in a healthier, more stable way. Honor your thoughts and allow them to come in the moment as they are, but redirect those old fears and hurts that keep you chained to the past.

When we're going through a hard time, it can seem impossible to find a balanced way to think. By reparenting ourselves we can find a path to happiness and acceptance. It just takes persistence.

4. Recognize your own emotional cruelty.

Dealing with ourselves harshly is a coping mechanism, and it's one that does more harm than good. When we're overly harsh on ourselves, we start to shy away from that inner monologue and look to others for reprieve. You can undo this pattern of self-criticism by finding a better way to deal with yourself and your emotions when the going gets tough.

Realize that there is genuine suffering in your life and accept that (sometimes) you are the cause of it. Accept that there's a better way and recognize that being hard on yourself is doing nothing but compounding your negative emotions. Recognizing our own emotionally cruelty can be a hard thing to do, but take a second look and you'll often see that you're your own worst enemy.

5. Identify and let go of self-destructive patterns.

Much of our neediness stems from the hard things that happened to us in our childhood or adolescence. By identifying these events and identifying better ways to respond to them, we can undo the hurts of the past and help stop the self-destructive patterns that do so much damage to our mental and physical wellbeing.

Exploring our past is the key to unlocking the hangups of right now.

There's no substitute for a good therapist, but you can do a lot of good just by opening up to yourself brutally and acceptingly. The aim is to learn how to let go of the past, rather than letting it define you. There's no one path to that, but there are a few techniques that can help.

The first is identifying the triggers that keep you linked negatively to the past. These are the behaviors, people or habits that bring up all the bad stuff that leave you feeling funky and unloved. When you know your triggers, you start to see the footfalls of the traps and can avoid them before you find yourself in catastrophe.

Learning how to identify triggers and patterns before they happen also allows us to let go of the illusions that are at the core of our emotional dependency. When you start to pull back the covers and see the reasons for your reactions, you start to see the world for the way it is rather than the way you want it to be. This is the secret to finding ourselves. We have to get on the same plane first, though, and that's often the hardest part.

6. Detachment as liberation.

The human mind is a master when it comes to convincing us that we need more than we actually do. This is true when it comes to our relationships as well, and that feeling of love that so many of us crave so desperately.

By coming to view detachment as a form of liberation, you can free yourself from the constant need to love and be loved. While desire is a thing that can often point us in the direction of the things that give us joy, it can be a dangerous bedfellow as well, leading us in the direction of things that destroy us rather than build us up.

Just because you have a desire for something does not mean it adds value to your life. When you see your desire as a part of yourself, you have no choice but to act. Seeing it removed from you, however, as an impulse that is basic to all animals — well, that can have some truly transformative powers all on its own.

It is possible to let go of our desires by deliberately shifting our focus away from those things that cause us to obsessively spiral into the "need trap". If our desires surge upon resistance, then take the time to sit down and address them and their foundations.

Detaching yourself from your desires is an interesting experience in choice; find the lines between what desires must be obeyed and what can be dismissed. The answer might surprise you.

7. Develop some patience.

Part of embracing your emotional independence is improving the skills and elevating the things you can actually do for yourself.

Developing skills takes time and it takes commitment and a resolution never to compromise yourself. Above all, though, it takes patience — because, as they say: "Rome wasn't built in a day."

Cultivate patience in your life and try to have a greater patience for the journey of life in general. It's not always smooth sailing, but there is always a smooth lining to any circumstance. The sooner you come to have this patience, the sooner you'll be able to get on with developing the skills you need to thrive on your own.

8. Let go of idealistic expectations.

Being emotionally dependent forces us to see the world in a very skewed way. When you're dependent on another person in this manner, you become more likely to make excuses for their poor behavior (or worse) make excuses for your own.

This naive idealism is required to exist in a world where only the external can make you happy. The biggest danger with this type of wishful thinking is that it forces us to pull the wool over own eyes and detach from reality.

Needing someone to be the right person for you makes it easy for you to disregard evidence to the contrary and can often result in keeping you chained to the things that are counterproductive to your growth or dangerous to mental and physical wellbeing.

While loyalty is a beautiful thing, delusion is not. To break free of your dependence on other people you have to start seeing things — and people — for what and what they really are, rather than what you want them to be.

Tips for letting go of false ideals: Stop confusing friendliness with friendship. Don't confuse casual friendship with loyalty. Stop doing favors with the assumption that those favours will be returned. Stop confusing romantic curiosity with romantic interest.

9. Stop confusing your needs with someone else's responsibilities.

No one else in the world is responsible for your happiness but you. While the attitudes of your childhood might have been dependent on your parents or guardians, the attitude you have from this moment forward depends on you.

One of the most important steps on our road in life in coming to accept that our needs are not someone else's responsibility. It's tempting to get angry when someone sells us short, but that's not the solution to getting where we need to go.

The real answers are in learning that there are limitations to every relationship; friendships and romantic entanglements included. You can ask for help all you want, or depend on someone to make you happy, but at the end of the day they can't give you something that they don't have.

Imaging that anyone "should" help you to feel better about yourself is a mistake of epic proportions. The longer you go living your life under this belief, the more miserable you will be. The sooner you face reality and face the fact that only you are responsible for your happiness, the more joy you will find in the little moments of your life.

10. Avoid letting your desire get carried away.

Desire is a powerful emotion and whether or not we know to avoid its pull, the temptation it offers can be too strong. We get carried away by our ideas of how life should be, and when we don't get the things we want the disappointment injures us.

Avoid this injury by refusing to let you desire get carried away.

Observe what it is that makes you go into such longing and develop the techniques you need to resist the temptations that don't suit your authentic self. Focus on a healthy sense of self-control by detaching yourself from unhealthy desires and the less-than-worthwhile acts they drive you to commit.

A common side effect of desire is fixation, but this obsession causes us to lose touch with the values that make us who we are. Stop the fixation before it starts by knowing your triggers and how to control them.

Tips for keeping your desire in check: Don't confuse childhood traumas or pain as someone being "right" for you. Don't confuse the feeling you get about someone with knowing who they actually are. Stop confusing attraction with a "healthy fit". Stop loving an impression of someone rather than who they really are.

11. Letting go of the need to control others.

Though we often confuse emotional dependent people with passive or submissive people, that isn't always the case. Those who are emotionally deponent can be just as manipulative and controlling as those who are not. It all comes down to letting go of this need for control.

The less you feel you are able to do for yourself, the more you will come to demand that others do those things for you. This can lead to emotional manipulation and an obsession with control that is damaging not only to ourselves but our loved ones as well.

Even if you have a noble reason for wanting to control someone else, manipulating the feelings and actions of another is wrong. Controlling other people is counterproductive to our happiness and actually pushes our partners away by forcing them to see us as the broken people that we are, unable to control ourselves or the way we feel about the things going on in our lives.

The behavior of others is unpredictable and uncontrollable. Seeking to make it otherwise brings nothing but more unhappiness to our lives. Drop your need to control and influence others by exerting that control and influence over yourself instead. If you can't control your own emotions and behaviors, after all, how the hell are you going to control it anyone else? (Trick question: you can't.)

Putting It All Togethe

Escaping the crutch of emotional dependence isn't easy, but it's necessary in order to find the strength we need to survive this crazy roller coaster ride called life.

It's possible to learn how to overcome our emotional dependency when stop to take a hard, honest look at the traumas and histories that make up who we are. By getting back in touch with our inner child and healing the injuries of the past, we can find who we are again and make some serious strides toward a future we can be proud of.

Letting go of our need for others is hard, and its even hard in a world that tells us we need external love in order to thrive. Drop that lie and have the courage to live bravely in your truth. There's a path to healing out there for you, but you have to be strong enough to walk it on your own.

CHAPTER 5

ADULT EMOTIONAL DEPENDENCY

Adult Emotional Dependency (AED) is a recently discovered mental condition, caused by the abnormal continuation in adulthood of Emotional Dependency.

The condition seems to affect a large segment of our actual society, and has shown to be the hidden root-cause of many forms of anxiety and fear. Some of the conditions associated with Adult Emotional Dependency (AED) are: generalized anxiety, unjustified feeling of unsafe, fear of judgement and rejection, need for approval, confidence issues, performance anxiety, social anxiety, starvation for love and attention, depression, alcohol and drugs abuse, addictions, feeling overwhelmed and tired, neediness or emotional numbness, poor performance and much more.

Adult Emotional Dependency (AED) symptoms

Our human nature is to become self-reliant and emotionally independent in adulthood. Emotionally independent individuals are able to interact freely and comfortably with partners, families, friends and community – from a place of equality and personal empowerment. This allows us to be socially inter-dependent, the ability to interact and share our lives with people by free choice - not constrained by fear and need.

On the contrary, emotional dependency in adulthood builds complex and painful layers of anxiety and fear and typically results in several debilitating emotions/feelings. Adult Emotional Dependency (AED) is the cause of the symptoms related to being emotionally dependent in adulthood upon 'others' (peers, colleagues, friends, family, partners, social environment - not necessarily upon a specific person - as source of protection, approval, leadership and emotional fulfillment. These may include:

Fear of:

- Judgment
- Rejection
- Abandonment

Belief in the need for:

- External leadership and/or validation
- Over-giving to being a 'pleaser'
- Accepting abuse to get affection

Feelings of:

- Self-doubt
- Neediness and self-focus
- Inadequacy
- Social anxiety
- Chronic insecurity
- Lacking an identity
- Being a fraud and a failure
- Being a child in a world of adults

- Resentment for the lack of external leadership and support

Emotional dependency throughout adult life creates:

- Anxiety
- Stress
- Addictions
- Feeling overwhelmed and tired
- Depression
- Dependency in relationships
- Starvation for love and attention
- Loneliness and solitude
- Loss of spirit-mind connection
- Panic attacks
- Chronic anger
- Unwarranted fears
- An inferiority complex
- Antisocial tendencies
- Emotional and spiritual numbness
- Borderline personality
- Unsuccessful personal life and relationships
- Unfulfilled artistic and professional aspirations

Because anxiety and fear use a large amount of brain resources, Adult Emotional Dependency (AED) massively overwhelms our brainpower thereby reducing our overall performance capabilities in every aspect of life, work, school and sport.

How to terminate Adult Emotional Dependency (AED)?

Adult Emotional Dependency (AED) terminates only if Emotional Self-Reliance is implemented. As soon the missing parental self-reliance models are acquired, Adult Emotional Dependency (AED) ceases and the connected emotional consequences are cleared. The emotional freedom produced by the termination of Adult Emotional Dependency (AED) , provides the ability to transform the needs produced by dependency to the autonomy of choice offered by interdependency; it also frees all the brainpower misused by Adult Emotional Dependency (AED) , which becomes available for high-performance, creativity and happiness.

A fast and natural solution to terminate Adult Emotional Dependency (AED) is offered by CognitiveOS Hypnosis®. A proven program that helps conquer emotional independence and release all unwanted layers of anxiety and fear. By clearing your mind and making inefficient behaviors built around dependency obsolete, your mind will redirect your brainpower towards creating efficient behaviors, performance, self-confidence, efficiency, clarity, and happiness.

The CognitiveOS Hypnosis® program provides an emotional framework that mimics the parental models needed to provide the confidence of self-leadership. Once the framework is in-place and the capacity for self-reliance is engaged, CognitiveOS Hypnosis® guides and trains your mind to clear away unwanted layers of anxiety and fears.

Within a couple of weeks of completing the program, daily feelings of isolation created by dependency are transformed into the ability to relate comfortably and inter-dependently, through the prism of choice and not need, with others. The effect is staggering – the isolation created by dependency is transformed to enjoyable inter-dependent relationships with others - where you finally see and enjoy the world around you without anxiety or fears, acting by choice instead of need. Obsolete behaviors built around dependency thus disappear – allowing the mind to redirect the reclaimed brainpower and use it to achieve higher levels of performance, efficiency and happiness in every area of your life.

Terminate Adult Emotional Dependency (AED) will allow you to:

- Become emotionally self-sufficient and independent.
- Transform dependency to interdependency.
- Enhance strengths and confidence – establishing leadership in the professional and personal life.
- Clear the real cause of addictions – taking control over life's events.
- Manage successfully thoughts, feelings and emotions.
- Enhance creative, academic, artistic and athletic performances.

- Spark attraction – experiencing fulfilling, happy and balanced relationships.

- Clear procrastination, getting things done – achieving life-long goals.

- Free your natural powers – gaining efficiency and success in every aspects of life.

- Establish an efficient spirit-mind alignment – accessing unconditional happiness.

- Fully capitalize on the therapeutic and self-development work done in the past, and the future efforts invested in personal development.

CHAPTER 6

HOW TO OVERCOME EMOTIONAL DEPENDENCY

Independence is generally a good thing. But believe it or not, there are folks who are inordinately and unhealthily independent: they're far too determined to do as they please, whenever they want. They feel entitled to set their own rules and are forever ignoring or contesting society's norms. They're determined not to be beholden to anyone or to subordinate themselves in any way to a "higher power" or authority. That can be a big problem, not only for relationships but for society as a whole. I've spent a professional lifetime studying and dealing with such individuals.

There are also folks who step in line and meet expectations far too easily and quickly. They tend be overly deferential, especially in their relationships. Again, problems arise because the balance is off. Some folks simply don't have enough independence of thought or action. This manner of coping provides the breeding ground for emotional dependency.

Emotional dependency evolves in an insidious way. Life presents us with many different challenges, and how we feel about ourselves and our ability to cope in large measure determines how we'll meet those challenges. If we're riddled with doubts about our ability to handle things successfully we might not even try, and when we fail to assert ourselves or throw in the towel too quickly or easily, we deny ourselves the opportunity for occasional success. A vicious cycle can then develop: every time we back down, give up, or give in, we only reinforce the notion that we simply can't accomplish our goals. Thinking that way only further impairs our already poor self-image. And that's precisely how emotional dependency develops. Having an impaired sense of both self-efficacy and self-worth can easily predispose a person to seek reassurance, approval and support from others whom they view as stronger, more capable, and more confident. All too often, those with these characteristics are among the overly independent individuals I described earlier. That's how abuse and exploitation can enter a relationship.

Emotional dependency becomes a big problem when one's sense of personal value and power is too wrapped up in the approval of another. Folks whose happiness, sense of security, and sense of worth is dependent upon the actions or sentiments of another tend to be chronically miserable and depressed. They have a sense of helplessness and hopelessness. Emotional dependency and depression often go hand-in-hand.

Overcoming emotional dependency is actually a fairly straightforward proposition — but that doesn't mean it's easy to do, especially when your self-image and confidence are both in the tank. The task is simple: do the very things you fear to do. Meet life's challenges head-on, even if you're not sure you can emerge victorious. In fact, give yourself permission in advance to fail. Instead of berating yourself for any mistakes you do make, make it a point profit from them, regarding every failure as a learning experience. In time, with consistent determination and self-assertion, even in the face of possible failure, you'll eventually experience your fair share of successes. And that will help you build not only your confidence but also a greater sense of personal strength and self-worth.

Folks struggling with emotional dependency tend to focus their attention externally, looking to external sources for approval and satisfaction of their emotional needs. So overcoming emotional dependency is largely a matter of re-directing one's focus internally. It's about spending some good, wholesome time with one's feelings. It's tending to one's basic wants and needs. It's about reflecting on one's own choices and the consequences of those choices. Of course, one has to do this benignly, without unproductive self-criticism or condemnation. In the end, it's about getting to know oneself better and figuring out how to amplify one's natural strengths and deal constructively with one's weaknesses. In short, it's about healthy self-love.

Emotionally dependent individuals are chronically at risk for entering into and remaining in abusive and exploitative relationships, and they're at risk for all sorts of unhealthy ways of self-medicating the chronic pain such relationships engender. But there is a way out, and it all starts with doing something — anything — different from the usual and learning from the consequences. In the end, folks get rescued from emotional dependency by turning to the very person they so long mistrusted, avoided, and neglected — themselves.

1. Avoid giving away responsibility for your happiness

People who aren't sure about how to look after themselves emotionally are more likely to reach out for someone else to do it for them. But no matter how good someone makes you feel, it's still a good idea to develop and preserve as much emotional self-reliance as you can rather than relying too much on them.

Developing this requires self-observation, learning and practice but eventually you will be able to take care of yourself in situations where you might normally depend on someone else. For example, if you feel sad, lonely, despairing or stressed out then you could experiment with different ways of making those feelings dissolve.

This realisation can also be quite useful when you're feeling needy. For example, if someone does not reply to a message then you might think "Why can't they just reply?" But then instead of sending a second message, you take a step back and say "Okay, maybe I don't want to be someone who pressures people like this".

2. Practise being there for yourself more often

We all have an innate need to connect with other people and it's worth developing good friendships and relationships. The answer is not to shut yourself off from the world, to imagine that you can be fully self-reliant, to commit to the existence of a hermit and to officially declare your independence from the rest of the human race.

However, it is important to learn how to look after yourself too. And the ironic thing about wanting to be less "needy" is that the solution is to recognize that your needs are very important and won't go away if you neglect or ignore them. Dependency is often the result of having your needs neglected and then neglecting them yourself.

Here are some of the main ways to take greater care of yourself emotionally:

- Recognize your needs and prioritize your serenity and well-being

- Manage your needs regularly and strategically like a business

- Practice savouring your alone time and exploring playfulness

- Embrace real interest, curiosity, learning, discovery and wonderment

- Find or create a support group where you can express feelings

- Develop a list of healthy coping strategies and distractions

- Consciously return to the present moment several times a day

- Work on a variety of different sources of joy and connection

- Do some regular physical exercise to make your body feel better

- Treat yourself every week but also do something for your future

- Explore your capacity for sincere enthusiasm more often

- Wallow in anything positive and savour anything that brings joy

- Practice self-motivation or self-inspiration on a regular basis

- And finally, never forget that wherever there is life there is hope

Of course, you won't always be able to do all of these things but you will often be able to do some of them and to gradually get better at both self-care and self-development over time. The priority is just being good to yourself, being genuinely kind, caring and helpful towards yourself in a way that you may not be used to at all.

Solitude is your greatest opportunity to explore all of this. Imagine if you decided to spend a few months in complete solitude, perhaps as part of a sponsored charity initiative. A good question to ask might be: "How could I make this phase of solitude peaceful, relaxing, healing, playful, constructive, meaningful or worthwhile?"

You would probably discover many surprising ways to amuse yourself, look after yourself and make yourself feel better: perhaps through calming meditation, movies, music, books, courses and interests or simply by going on long walks accompanied by your imagination. Make it your project to explore and repeat what works for you.

3. Really get to know your vulnerable self

Pushing away your feelings and thoughts creates a void where self-connection could be. A great way to fill that void is to practice expressing yourself through spontaneous voice recording, writing or journaling. Getting to know yourself through a process of authentic self-expression is how you can start to make friends with yourself.

We often want other people to listen to us, to understand us and to support us because we have given up on the possibility of doing that for ourselves. Discovering who we are through an experimentally honest, raw and unedited expression of our true thoughts and feelings is a very good first step to self-understanding.

We feel helpless when we are not able to express ourselves. Describing your needs, desires, frustrations, hurt, fear, sadness, shame, despair, stressful irritation and anger about what isn't fair is a great way of giving yourself power so that you can be aware of what you are going through and help yourself in a spirit of self-compassion:

It's important to allow yourself to be as vulnerable as you truly feel inside and to express that vulnerability without reacting against yourself for being human. This means allowing yourself not only to express frustrations but also to say really helpless things such as "I'm scared that I just won't be able to cope" or "My heart is breaking".

The key to unlocking your self-compassion is to admit how hard what you are going through is. When expressing this, you may find yourself crying a little and feeling a sense of emotional release, which is wonderfully healing. It takes practice but it's worth working on this regularly, maybe with the help of some emotionally inspiring music.

Even if your emotions appear to be numbed by a harsh sense of being removed from reality, it's good to write about the confusion and despair that this makes you feel. Eventually, you can learn to fully sense your emotions and you will realize that there is really nothing more beautiful, innocent or adorable than your own heart.

As well as expressing feelings, it's good to write down your helpless thoughts so that you understand and can truly engage with your own mind. When you ignore your thoughts they are more likely to control you subconsciously. When you express them, you can start to deal with them more compassionately, rationally and responsively.

4. Practice loving self-parenting

Expressing vulnerability is a way of getting in touch with the part of you which is known as the inner child. The best way to empathize with and express that part of you is to identify with and speak directly as the inner child, saying things like "I feel really sad / hurt / scared / lonely right now" with real vulnerability in your voice.

Once you have sensed and genuinely expressed your helplessness, it's good to respond to that part of yourself from a perspective of loving parental attention. The first thing you can do is to simply notice how adorably innocent, vulnerable and blameless2 the inner child is when expressing suffering and take a few deep breaths.

When doing this, it may help to visualize and gently connect with a mental image of how you looked at a very young age. You can then say something compassionately accepting to softly reassure your inner child that it is okay to think or feel that way. After all, you cannot help what helpless thoughts and feelings occur to you and so:

You can then resolve to help yourself with loving intention. At this point, you are expressing yourself as the responsible adult who is determined to do their best to take care of their adorable child. Even if you don't know what to do, you can gently say "We'll figure this out" or perhaps go further and make a promise such as.

You could follow this up with a statement of helpful action, such as "Okay, we're going to do lots of deep breathing and relaxing. We're going to have the most soothing cup of tea ever brewed. We're going to watch that TV show! And slowly but surely, we're going to let go of all the silly things that have caused you all that terrible pain".

You can take a similar self-parenting approach to dealing with future challenges. For example, you might say "I know you're afraid/anxious. I know that this won't be easy. But I am here to do whatever I can to help you get through this situation. I know that everything is going to be okay because we can find a way to handle this".

And so, we have a process for dealing with your thoughts and emotions. First, you can allow yourself to fully express them with authentic vulnerability. Then, you can respond with compassionate acceptance and understanding. Finally, you can express a loving intention to deal with them in a kind and helpful way.

Even if some of your thoughts seem silly, remember that it's okay to have thoughts like that. You won't help your inner child by dismissing, rejecting, censoring or punishing such thoughts so allow them, fully express them and listen to them with all your heart before even considering whether it might be possible to think differently.

When you're going through a hard time, you may not always find a perfectly rational or balanced way to think about everything. But that's okay because any thought experienced while suffering is still a valid expression of emotional needs, frustrations or pain which above all require your sincere and humane acknowledgment.

5. Let go of attachments by focusing on gentle, deep breathing

Whenever you depend on someone or something, your mind has become deeply attached to that person or object. Your relationship with anything you strongly resist or desire is one of intense involvement or engagement. And so, the solution is to practice becoming detached or disengaged while staying in the present moment.

Sometimes, we find ourselves caught up in an inner world of mental attachments and reactions. We know this is happening when we start obsessing about a person, issue or situation, helplessly swept away by a chain of intense, related thoughts and emotions which signify that our suffering is stuck in "replay mode".

The best way to let of anything is to let go of everything, to change your focus so much that you give your mind a much-needed break from trying to control or cling onto anything or anyone. You can do this by focusing so much on your breath that the focus on everything else apart from the breath and body eventually starts to slide away.

It helps to find somewhere quiet to sit, gradually slowing down your breathing and starting to focus only on your breath. Of course, you will still become momentarily distracted by thoughts, feelings, sights, smells and sounds but you can gently acknowledge these and then come back to focusing only on your breath and body.

Whenever you feel as though you are being swept away by life's chaos or craziness, you can return to gently slowing down your breathing for a while. But it's also a good idea to spend at least fifteen minutes a day in sustained focus on gentle, deep breathing because this creates a calm space that can free your mind.

What you are doing in that space is allowing yourself to relax a little despite how the rest of the world can be. Letting go of all mental clinging and reacting helps you to realize that it is not worth going back to being too involved with what might not be good for you anyway and that you can't be bothered with that anymore.

6. Recognize self-harshness as a form of emotional cruelty

If you are used to dealing with yourself harshly then you probably developed this habit as a coping mechanism to deal with extreme circumstances. But self-harshness is best viewed as "inner child abuse", a form of emotional sadism that a part your mind has been secretly getting away with in the absence of compassionate oversight.

The key to overcoming this is to realize that your inner child genuinely suffers, therefore must be essentially innocent and does not deserve any of the harsh punishments that you have habitually put yourself through. You will need many years of kind and nurturing self-support so that you can recover, heal, grow and develop.

A good way to take responsibility for your self-harshness is to keep a list of the kinds of things you say, think and do to yourself that might be harsh. You can then ask whether each of these reactions is fair and helpful, whether you would do the same to someone you loved and whether you could replace it with a better response.

It's especially important to watch out for suppressive thoughts and reactions. We often punish ourselves for thinking or feeling a certain way, for example by responding with "Don't be silly" or "I shouldn't feel this way". It's far more helpful to encourage your inner child to say whatever is on their mind and to fully embrace that.

Just imagine if you met a lost child in the street. The child is afraid, sad, lonely, despairing, upset, angry or helpless in some other way. Would it be helpful to ignore the child or tell them to "Shut up"? Or would it be more helpful to listen to the child, be present with them, try to understand them and embrace their genuine concerns?

This is why making friends with yourself begins with being able to express and listen to your inner child. The part of you that struggles the most is the part that most needs to express itself, be acknowledged and feel understood. You are in the best and most proximate position to provide that understanding but it starts with self-expression.

7. Avoid confusing your needs with anyone's responsibility

An important step along the road to freedom is allowing other people to be completely free rather than holding onto open or secretive resentments about their behaviour. It may be tempting to get angry with someone who isn't there for you during a crisis or lets you down in some way but it isn't the real solution to your situation.

Consider how many times you may have passed a homeless person in the street and not even thrown them some loose change. When you become an "emotional beggar" you're in a similarly difficult situation. You can ask for help but there's just no point demanding it because the harsh truth is that nobody really owes you anything.

Part of the solution is simply accepting that people have natural limitations when it comes to friendships, relationships, humanity and understanding. They may find it hard enough to stay positive as it is already without having to look after those who have not yet learned to look after themselves, albeit through no fault of their own.

Imagining that anyone "should", "must" or "needs to" help you when they haven't explicitly agreed to do so can come across as manipulative because it confuses your needs with their responsibility. It's not worth testing anyone's limits by pressuring them to be someone they may not even be capable of becoming.

8. Recognize and let go of self-destructive childhood patterns

A lot of neediness may stem from difficult events that happened during childhood or adolescence. Identifying these events and the way you responded to them as a child is a great way to recognize why you may have got stuck in a place of emotional dependency and helplessness. The future does not have be like the past.

You don't want to get lost in the past but exploring it to some extent can help you to let go of patterns of thought, feeling and behaviour that you may have formed when you had no idea how to deal with what was going on. It's good to avoid "re-living" the same story over and over again by discovering new ways of responding.

There is probably no substitute for a good therapist because it really helps when you grow through a relationship with a responsible parent-like figure who knows what is best for you and can help you in a far less conditionally caring way. But in the long run, the aim is to let go of the past rather than letting it control your reactions.

Part of the solution is distinguishing between present situations and past situations they may remind you of. You can also distinguish between the helpless child you once were and the increasingly self-calming, self-soothing, self-caring, self-understanding, self-approving, self-nurturing and politely assertive adult you're becoming.

You may identify certain "triggers" that made you feel helplessly attached or seemed to make an old reaction necessary. You can then start seeing similar things as an invitation to a trap which you don't have to fall into rather than as something irresistible or impossible to ignore and which inevitably pulls you into deeper dependency.

This can also help you to recognize and let go of illusions at the core of the dependency. An example might be feeling a need to take responsibility for someone else's problems or well-being. Another might be believing that your survival depends on securing one person's approval or affection even at an unreasonable price3.

A common pattern in people raised by controlling parents is the idea that they have to do what someone else wants just because that person is upset or just because they are behaving in a cold or unreasonable manner. Patterns like this often result in the unhealthy suppression of healthy anger and a lack of assertiveness.

9. Recognize and manage any reckless impulsivity

Emotional dependency can create intense, overwhelming and confusing emotions. Reacting impulsively to that internal state can be very dangerous. What suddenly seems like a great idea when you're in a "reactive" mood could turn out to be a really bad idea and so it's worth recognizing and stepping back from that.

It's common to react to emotional overwhelm either by thinking "I can't tolerate this for a single second" or "Oh God, this is me now and I will feel like this forever". The good news is that neither of these automatic beliefs is true because feeling awful is a process which may have a few ups and downs but will eventually run its course.

Once you feel a lot calmer then you can think things through carefully. But feeling needy, upset, sad, stressed, angry, manic, tired, bored, hungry, low, high or drunk isn't a great basis for drawing important conclusions or making big decisions. To avoid consequences you may regret, it's good to heed the advice of Winston Churchill: "If you're going through hell, keep going".

When you're in the grip of intense feelings it can seem as if they will never go away. But the truth is that they always do when you give them enough time. This is why people often remind themselves that "This too shall pass" and wait it out rather than doing anything reckless to escape what they need to go through anyway.

The irony is that desperately reacting to make feelings go away often escalates problems with people. Rather than becoming involved in a potentially never-ending cycle of drama, it's better to express any intense feelings through private emotional journaling until you are in a fully recovered position to communicate far more carefully.

Whilst it can be good to express some feelings and needs to others, you can do so in combination with compassionate understanding, sympathetic attention and loving speech. And of course, it's important to sympathize with yourself too in case you are just too overwhelmed to be quite so diplomatic.

10. Recognize when you start being too clingy

A bit of adventurous self-introspection can help you to identify patterns of dependency in your thoughts or behaviour that you can work on overcoming. An example might be having an attitude of wanting "all or nothing" from people instead of truly appreciating whatever is freely offered in a spirit of sincere gratitude.

Signs of premature attachment may include a feeling of giddiness or sentimentality, a possessive sense of wanting to have someone all to yourself, a dream-like desire to "merge" and a tendency to fantasise. None of these things have to be a problem but you could be leading yourself on by getting a little ahead of yourself.

You may also recognise how you start thinking about what you want so that you can nip some of that dependent thinking in the bud at early stages. Spending too much time or energy focusing on what might be good for you may seem positive, exciting or inspiring but it can be dangerous for one reason. As C.S. Lewis put it: "Do not let your happiness depend on something you may lose"4

If you're getting to know someone new then another sign that you may be over-attaching is that you seem to be a lot more involved with them than they are with you. Even if you cannot help being more interested than them, you can help your level of involvement and it may be a good idea to roughly match about the same level as theirs.

We might call this the principle of healthy reciprocation. One of my personal slogans in life is "I'm not keen on people who aren't keen on me". This way of thinking is useful because it stops me from wasting too much time or energy on people who through no fault of their own cannot truly understand or appreciate what I have to offer.

If you start attaching to anyone too soon then you're prematurely giving them a degree of importance to you which they may not yet deserve. And so, you may need to give both yourself and them more distance to avoid overvaluing your interaction with them. The sooner you realise this risk the easier it is to avoid being clingy.

11. Avoid getting carried away by desire

It's easy to get carried away by the idea of wanting things to be a certain way. It starts with a mild preference but then it gets twisted in the mind, going through several stages:

"That might be nice" → "That couldn't possibly be bad for me" → "This must be good for me" → "This will make me happy" → "I'm starting to feel strangely unhappy without it" → "Nothing else could make me happy" → "Without it I might be devastated" → "I'm starting to feel unhappy, that just proves how much I need it" → "I need it so much that nothing else exists anymore"

Part of the solution is to observe what makes you go deeper into such longing. For example, if you meet someone new then you may find that looking into their eyes a lot or focusing on their body makes you feel a little physically addicted and so doing less of that will help you to stay detached rather than getting carried away by possibilities.

Avoiding alcohol in these situations is also likely to help. As soon as you recognise that something could make you more addicted then the solution is to want less of it rather than more of it. This is because what you really want is to avoid losing your usual healthy self-control in the process of being swept away by desire.

A very common psychological aspect of romantic desire is fixation, an obsessive or exclusive focus on a particular person or thing. Without realising it, you may be fixating on someone by imagining that they might be "the one" instead of merely "one of a kind" and appealing in many ways but not necessarily right for you at all.

Another aspect of far-fetched desire could be the illusion of immediate urgency, the rather impatient sense that something has to happen right now or really soon. A desire for instant gratification may be a habit or simply a result of wanting to escape how you feel rather than dealing with it. But it might be better to say: "Something along those lines would great at some point but I can survive without it just fine for now"

This allows you to avoid fixating by broadening rather than narrowing the focus of your desire. Rather than thinking "Oh Henry! When oh when will you be mine?", you will feel calmer if you conclude "Yep, what this feeling about Henry shows is that it might be good to meet a nice man at some point, perhaps one a little like Henry".

Fixation is what makes people feel insecure about whether they will get what they have persuaded themselves they "must" have. A better way to view many encounters is like playing the lottery. There is no reason to take it seriously just because the stakes are high. The mistake is being "determined to win" when luck is involved.

That doesn't mean that everything we try comes down to luck but it's still best to view life's opportunities as a series of games. You can eventually win one of those games especially if you accept that skill and effort are also required but the element of luck in any individual game is usually far too big to justify fixating on its outcome.

Another way to stop yourself from getting carried away is to be mindful of any tendency to fantasise. Even if you experienced a good connection with someone, it may not have meant as much to them. And while you are building things up in your imagination, they may have already gone back to their life and forgotten all about it.

What may seem completely amazing and the answer to all your problems may turn out to be surprisingly bad for you. And yet desperation has a way of making things look very different, urgent and unquestionable. It's easy to get swayed by first impressions about new people and to forget that all that glitters is not gold. You might:

- Confuse being attracted to someone with them being right for you

- Confuse a feeling with genuine sexual and emotional compatibility

- Confuse a strong crush or visual attraction with a deeper attraction

- Confuse infatuation or obsession with really knowing and loving a person

- Confuse a feeling you get from someone with knowing what they are like

- Confuse your first few impressions with what someone is really like

- Confuse how someone first presents themselves with what they are really like

- Confuse loving an impression of someone with loving who they really are

- Confuse insecurity, emptiness, loneliness or wishful thinking with love

- Confuse a fear of "abandonment" with someone being right for you

- Confuse childhood traumas or pain with someone being right for you

It's also very easy to confuse a beautiful moment of deep connection with the idea that your friendship with someone has "progressed to the next level". People can be fickle, relationships have their ups and downs and even when intimacy feels good it may bring up unexpected issues that eventually create greater distance.

It's not quite correct to believe that someone or something can "make me happy" even if they become your main source of joy. What's happening is that you are making your happiness depend on them and that dependency can make you unhappy. The more you focus on what you think "makes" you happy the more you start to depend on it.

You can even recognise and let go of neediness in your everyday thoughts. Changing your language is one way to tackle that. Instead of saying "I need to" you might start saying "I'd like to". Instead of saying "I need this" you might say "I would love that if it were possible". You might start to think of any expectation as a mere preference.

12. View detachment from desire as a form of self-liberation

Whilst it's absolutely vital to look after our basic needs, one of the dangers of the human condition is that the mind can always persuade us that we don't have enough and that we need more. Desire can become insatiable and this often happens fairly soon after we get exactly what we imagined would bring us lasting satisfaction5.

Some of our desires might be viewed as a kind of inner tyrant, dictator or slave-driver6 who tells us what to do in the most unreasonably forceful way. It may sometimes be possible to detach by observing these inner demands as if they were coming from outside, for example by picturing a madman screaming "You must want this!"

However, it's better to recognise that this part of your mind does have a positive intention: it only wants what it genuinely believes will be best for you7. And so, you can view it with compassion and understanding while also viewing it as external to your true self and recognising that its insistence may be a little misguided and unhelpful.

When you see your desire as part of yourself then you have almost no choice but to act on it since you simply see it as "what I want". But when you see your desire as something outside of yourself which is pressuring you to do something then you have more of a chance to free yourself of any slavish or unquestioning subservience to it.

Some of our most basic impulses might be viewed as a result of the process of natural selection. They are geared towards doing whatever it takes to pass our genes onto the next generation9. However, there are many examples of situations where blindly following these impulses does not help us or others to live fulfilling lives.

A simple example might someone attending a social event in the hope of making a good friend. On their right is another nice person who shares lots of common interests with them. On their left is someone who they would not even get on with but whom they find very physically attractive. Which way are they more likely to focus?

Their feelings might urge them to look left even though focusing on the other person is more likely to be good for their long term well-being. This is because feelings are often used to trick us into doing whatever serves natural selection10. It's rather like being hypnotised or fooled by a master who does not really care about us at all.

Sometimes, it's possible to let go of desire by deliberately shifting our focus away. But when resisting only makes desire stronger then it may help to calmly observe or examine11 its pressuring for a while and to detach by viewing it as an interesting experience outside of ourselves rather than as an internal command which has to be obeyed.

13. Recognise and let go of any refusal to be happy

We all sometimes experience a feeling which, on a subconscious level, might be explained in terms of a child jumping up and down and screaming "I want my ice cream!" The child may seem spoilt but it's more likely that they are very distressed and genuinely believe that ice cream is what they must have to feel okay again.

To any adult observing the scene, it is obvious that the child could be okay even without any ice-cream. And so it is important to observe the child within yourself and to recognise when you might be holding your own well-being to ransom by insisting on something you can survive without because this inner tantrum can become life-ruining.

Again, it's important to do this with compassion. Your inner child is tired of all that pain and distress and believes that the answer is to fight for what it wants. That's completely understandable and so it's important to respond with kindness because that is what is really needed. Only once you have done this can you let go of the demand.

It's worth remembering that we can often experience great moments of relaxation or joy without needing to have some special reason for feeling good. But, of course, when we get carried away with desire, a part of the mind may start refusing to feel okay without having something which it believes we must have to be happy.

Being okay without what you wanted doesn't mean that you've given up on your hopes and dreams. It just means that you are willing to make the most of any situation, even when it's not what you would have preferred. And in some ways, that flexible attitude could be seen as the secret of true happiness, serenity or well-being.

Instead of thinking "What have I got to be so happy about?", it's better to embrace the idea of relaxing just for the sake of it and of being joyful just for the sake of it. Allowing yourself to feel okay whenever possible and in spite of the way circumstances are is what makes you less dependent on them and it's worth being specific about this.

Identifying what you have recently made your well-being rely on can be an eye opener. For example, a troubling thought like "People are driving me crazy!" may be true to some extent. But it could also be reinterpreted as "I insist that everyone around me is great" which is clearly a little overdependent and unrealistic.

Another example might be "Nothing is making any sense!" which is another way of saying "I insist that everything always makes sense" and is not strictly necessary. Recognising which arbitrary conditions you keep placing on your own serenity can increasingly set your mind free and improve your resilience through greater flexibility.

14. Practise letting go of the need to control others

The less you are able or willing to do for yourself, the more empty you are likely to feel on the inside and the more tempted you may then be to control other people so that they can do things for you instead. For this reason, emotionally dependent people very often struggle with a related addiction to controlling other people12.

Even if you have a noble reason for wanting to influence someone, trying to limit their freedom is likely to have a negative effect on how they perceive you. They may come to associate you with an uncomfortable sense of being manipulated or pressured into doing something against their will and may even start to secretly dislike you.

Some of our thoughts may be disguised forms of control based on what we incorrectly believe we must have. Here are some examples of what we may be unknowingly insisting upon in certain situations. The solution is to recognise if we are secretly making a demand and to transform it into a slightly more gentle preference or request.

- "I'm so lonely!" > but I may be insisting on company now

- "I need you!" > but I may be insisting on having you here now

- "I don't need this!" > I may be insisting that this be otherwise

- "You don't need to say that!" > I may be insisting that you don't say that

- "You need to do this!" > I may be insisting that you do this

Of course, these statements may be expressions of valid concerns and do not always translate into unknowingly suppressed demands. But a good sign that you are in fact being rather too forceful, controlling, demanding, insistent or "pushy" is that you feel an accompanying physical "pushing" sensation of pressure within your body.

It's also possible to feel a "pulling" sensation which often signifies that some form of resistance is causing us to insist on what we think we need. For example, if you subconsciously believe that you might die or be utterly helpless unless you get what you want then your insistence is likely to be driven by that resistant belief.

Part of the solution is to recognise that people's behaviour is often as unpredictable or uncontrollable as the weather. That's not always the case but it's important to be able to recognise when it is and step aside. You may feel sad because you were hoping for sunshine but that doesn't mean that it's worth getting angry with the rain.

However, an equally important part of the solution is to acknowledge anger whenever it arises. Rather than suppressing anger and allowing it to control you subconsciously, it's better to consciously recognise whenever you feel angry and to allow yourself to feel it fully because this gives you more of a choice about what to do with it.

A good way to make friends with anger is to say "I feel angry about this – and that's okay". Recognising that anger is totally understandable and neither good nor bad then allows you to say "Now, I have a choice: I can either do something reasonable to try to improve this situation or I can try to let go and come to terms with how it is".

Anger is there to let you know that something isn't good for you and to provide you with a burst of powerful energy which urges you to take action. But when there is nothing you can realistically do to improve the situation then you can free yourself of the need to control it by channelling that energy into a promise to take better care of yourself.

15. Recognise when your inner reactions make you more dependent

In addition to insisting too much on some things, dependent people often have an overly dependent attitude of resistance. It's easy to believe that something might be intolerable, unmanageable or awful when in reality it could be handled. Such unnecessary dread-making resistance can cause as much suffering as unnecessary insistence.

Whenever we think we need something, we are more likely to start imagining that not having it might be an emergency. We might start thinking of the situation as more serious, important, drastic or catastrophic than it needs to be. And that makes us more likely to insist on something rather than being gentle and easygoing.

Part of the solution is to practise getting things in proportion. A lot of challenging situations can be thought of as "annoying rather than awful", "stressful but not unmanageable" or "a pity but not necessarily a tragedy". Some people can be thought of as "not very nice but hardly Adolf Hitler". A good question to ask might be: "Is my resistance / insistence making things worse in this situation?"

Variations might include "Is my excessive vigilance / imagination / drasticising / awfulising / horrorising13 / intolerance / closed-minded aversion / demonising / fixation on disaster / impatience / inflexibility / over-certainty / greed / asking too much / over-seriousness / over-involvement / perfectionism / fixating making things worse?"

That doesn't mean that you should start criticising yourself as soon as you feel distressed. As I've already said, it's important to put self-kindness first. But once you have fully expressed, sympathised with and soothed yourself then it may be worth considering whether any unnecessary resistance or insistence played a role in your distress.

I'm not suggesting that a sense of insistence or resistance is always a bad thing because it could inspire us to take genuinely reasonable action to improve a situation for ourselves or others. But it's always worth recognising when an internal attitude of excessive resistance or insistence creates suffering by making things worse.

We may insist or resist too much because our minds give something the wrong meaning. For example, you may subconsciously believe that you can only be okay if someone likes you or that if they don't like you then that "must mean" that you are awful. Giving any situation a drastic meaning like that can also make you more dependent.

16. Take responsibility for dependent beliefs and attitudes

It's very easy to suddenly become psychologically addicted to anything, such physical intimacy and external attention, kindness, sympathy, companionship or approval. Nobody can blame themselves when this happens because they often do so without fully realising the precise role that they played in making that happen.

If you start telling yourself that you "need" something then this is likely to significantly alter your mental reality. You can persuade yourself of anything but it's good to take responsibility for doing so. When you depend on something, your mind creates its own special system of self-reward and self-punishment around it.

For example, I could keep telling myself over and over again that I "need" to see a black cat run across the street. If I genuinely start believing that, hoping for it and building my dreams around it then this will affect my emotions. If I see see the black cat then I may even feel blissful because I finally got what I thought I really needed.

I could say that the black cat "makes" me happy but it's not really true. I made my happiness depend on it by strongly persuading myself it was what I most needed in the world. I rewarded myself with wish-fulfilling happiness at seeing the black cat and punished myself with a sense of frustration and disappointment if I didn't see it.

If you do this with a person then you have turned them into kind of object, a mental object known as the object of desire. You might not really know what they are like but your imagination has seized upon the possibility that they could be good for you and this mere possibility can be enough to drive our silly brains wild with anticipation.

17. Challenge popular cultural assumptions about the nature of love

We may feel supported by personal, cultural or popular prejudices that seem to "confirm" some kind of value in sliding down the slippery slope of dependency. Falling "head over heels" and "madly in love" may seem "thrilling", "caring" or "destined" rather than risky, unwise and merely a sign of preceding loneliness14 or self-neglect.

It's easy to forget that "romantic" songs, books and movies often involve a somewhat naive and teenage glorification of unhealthy neediness. Dependency creates strong and addictive emotions but, as beautiful as healthy love can be, such imbalanced longing is not something that needs to be idealised or seen as magical.

The danger of being romantic is that it may cause you to want to fall in love with someone, whether or not loving them will be good for you and whether or not your feelings will be returned. Romance wants you to become addicted and presents the state of being addicted as something beautiful for which people should strive.

18. Take people off their silly pedestals

Common themes in dependency include low self-esteem and a lack of assertiveness. This could be caused by a number of different factors but it is commonly the result of people being taught at a very young age that they are not fully allowed to express themselves, to assert themselves or simply to be the person they really are.

Children who are emotionally harmed in some way usually have no choice but to accept what is being done to them. They are in a natural position of both physically and mentally looking up to those who neglect or mistreat them. When they grow up, they then carry this model of child-like helplessness with them wherever they go.

This can result in a tendency to agree too much, to empathise too much, to give too much or to make too many excuses for the aggressive or manipulative behaviour of others. The best way to cultivate self-respect is to start respecting yourself, which means respecting your own feelings, needs, views, rights and personal boundaries.

Even if you sometimes feel worthless, never forget that you are an equally deserving member of society with a right to the same respect, dignity and consideration as anyone else. It's important to notice and diplomatically but firmly let people know when you disagree or when something isn't good for you. I call this "the power of no".

Here are some of the things that emotionally mistreated children need to unlearn:

- I'm essentially wrong so whatever others say must be right

- I'm worthless so I must treat others as more worthy than me

- I'm bad or guilty so others get to be the supreme judge of me

- I have no rights so others have a right to walk all over me

- My needs aren't important so I have to do whatever others need

- My problems aren't important so I have to take on other people's problems

- I am low and all the way down here so others are way high up there

Reversing such beliefs will be a great step to better assertiveness. You are no longer a helpless child but rather an adult survivor willing to develop a sense of being able to effectively manage situations by being vocal, expressive, honest, direct, straightforward, calm, clear, firm, friendly, mature, persuasive, responsive and resourceful.

You can also give yourself power by viewing unreasonable behaviour from an independent position of critical disagreement and self-respecting fairness. If anyone behaves aggressively or manipulatively, secretly look down on what they are doing as rather pathetic, ridiculous, immature, clueless and unknowingly self-embarassing.

You may not have to look down at the person because there could be valid causal reasons why they are ignorant, confused, thoughtless or disturbed. But it's still important to recognise any serious problem or threat in their behaviour and to deal with it in an assertive and balanced way that can realistically improve things for you.

19. Work on developing an authentically independent mindset

When you think about it, children "individuate" partly through disagreement. Occasionally saying no makes you an individual rather than a total conformist or slave. And so, when it comes to almost any issue always ask "What do I actually think about this?" rather than immediately deferring to what anyone else might happen to think.

Many emotionally dependent people will sometimes automatically view themselves from someone else's viewpoint. For example, if someone else is being unfair towards them then they may over-empathise with that unfair person's perspective and forget that it's far more important to form their own independent viewpoint.

If a person's dependency was caused by a bad parent then they will often keep viewing themselves from that bad parent's perspective. The solution is to start a late teenage rebellion by disagreeing with the bad parent who now exists mainly in their own head. You can replace these outdated views with better ones based partly on kindness: "From now on, I am the one who decides what I think about things".

This means taking your view of yourself into your own hands and doing so in a spirit of fairness and consistency. For example, if you would never judge someone else for being in the same situation as yourself then there is equally no need to make a harsh exception by judging yourself for being in that situation either.

It also means that you can start daring to disagree with other people more often, not just for the sake of disagreeing but for the sake of being faithful to your true self. Wearing a mask just to please others can be humorously accepted as necessary in some situations but it is usually best viewed as a form of self-betrayal.

This doesn't mean that your aim should be to start unnecessary wars or put yourself in harm's way. But better assertiveness often begins with allowing yourself to honestly disagree, noticing when you disagree and being willing to express disagreement calmly and reasonably, no matter who someone else may think they are.

One of the reasons why some dependent people wear a mask is that they fear rejection but all they succeed in getting others to accept is a mask. Learning to express your true self at a support group can help you to build up the confidence and ability to get more of the real social acceptance which your true self wants and deserves.

So much of psychology is just about allowing yourself simply to be who you already are. You may think of yourself as the problem but you are actually the solution. And the more you realise that being yourself is the solution, the less you will feel as if you need to depend on other people's permission or approval just to be yourself.

20. Develop a greater sense of assertive responsibility

If you are not used to being assertive then you may be accustomed to viewing many problems in terms of other people's behaviour rather in terms of your ability to respond. For example, if someone misunderstands you then you might focus on how unfair they are being rather than seeing that as an opportunity to explain yourself.

When the idea of standing up for yourself seems strange or scary then you get used to having a very passive and defeatist mentality which assumes that other people can simply walk all over you and that there is nothing you can do about it. This may trigger understandably helpless feelings of anxiety, fear, despair, anger or even hatred.

If you assume that you are a powerless victim then your whole focus is likely to become preoccupied with what other people do and how they make you feel. In other words, your emotions are likely to depend on their behaviour almost as if they have a magical remote control that can make you upset whenever they choose.

You may find yourself constantly reacting15 to other people by saying things like "I just can't believe he did that!", "What on earth is her problem? or "Why can't they just understand?" The solution is to let go of excessive control, to allow people to be unreasonable but to start responding reasonably and assertively to their unreasonableness.

This does not mean that you will always get a good or fair result because outcomes can never be dictated. But even when you lose out in one of life's series of games, it still feels good to play well by standing up for yourself in an optimistic but also realistic and undemanding way which allows people to have their flaws and differences.

Being independent is not just about self-care but also about a willingness to learn how to make moves and deal with challenges to try and improve your circumstances. Rather than obsessing about how bad a problem or situation is, your focus can switch to how you can handle it or how you can actively make make things better.

Realising how much power you can reasonably wield as an adult allows you to gradually replace the outdated model of childhood helplessness with a more hopeful and engaged outlook on life. The new assumption is that taking effective action is usually possible and can transform many negative situations into positive ones.

A good way to take a more active approach to meeting your needs is to set goals. For example, if you have a thought like "I never seem to make friends" then you could make it a goal to go to more social events. If you then think "Nobody says hi to me", you could make it your goal to introduce yourself to at least two people every time.

The point is that you are no longer sitting back and depending on other people to improve things for you. Rather, you see it as your job to take reasonable action to increase the chances of improving your circumstances. In this way, setting goals can help you to take a more active and effective approach to just about any need or issue16.

21. Cultivate an easygoing sense of self-respect

Many dependent people live with a partly subconscious sense of being essentially flawed or defective to the very core of their being. They suspect that there is something not merely imperfect but fundamentally wrong with them and they depend on other people to deliver them from this rather drastic and far-fetched self-judgment.

This may lead to a compulsive habit of trying to secure external approval by proving themselves to be special or worthy. They may do this by chasing self-improvement, recognition, greatness, perfection or superiority in an area such as work, fitness, education, artistic ability, personal charm, moral image or physical appearance.

It may also result in a heightened sensitivity to the slightest possible implication of rejection. It's as if they are always ready to doubt their basic human worth and reject themselves unless someone else makes them feel admired and desired because the core suspicion that they are shamefully terrible never goes away.

Part of the solution is to humanely reject the idea of being somehow "fatally flawed". It's completely normal for any human being to have a whole bunch of flaws and to make all kinds of mistakes. And having more problems to deal with than people who have been emotionally privileged in life doesn't mean that you are the problem.

Another way of tackling the issue is to understand the belief as a symptom of brainwashing. At some point, many of us have had the unpleasant experience of being treated more like an object than a person. But it's important to recognise if you learnt to copy rather than renounce this ignorant and inhumane attitude towards yourself.

If you look up to people who are not good for you then you may end up placing your self-approval in their hands, giving them the authority to act like a supreme judge who gets to make a binding decision as to whether or not you are okay. There is no need to outsource your self-acceptance to anyone, let alone to inconsiderate fools.

Self-respect doesn't need to be about admiring yourself. It can simply mean respecting your needs and feelings as a person. Not even the worst insult, criticism, rejection or shaming experience can stop you from being essentially okay because being okay comes with being human and nothing can ever take away your humanity.

All self-esteem means is admitting and appreciating that you have some good points. But you don't need to depend on self-esteem to be kind, friendly, caring or humane towards yourself. It's enough simply to remember that you are a real person and that it's never worthwhile, fair or necessary to have a problem with yourself.

22. Avoid idealising anyone

The more we idealise, the deeper we sink into the quicksand of desire. The more you imagine anything to be perfect or put anyone on a pedestal the more you are setting yourself up for both addiction and almost inevitable disappointment. What seems like the Holy Grail can easily turn out to be more like a poisoned chalice.

Worshipping anyone as if they are some kind of "saviour" or "Messiah" figure is particularly dangerous. Imagining that someone has a supernatural ability to make you whole18 is really a way of persuading yourself that there's something you can't live without and that you could never feel okay or develop yourself independently.

It may seem like idealising someone is a great compliment but you're not doing yourself or them any favours. Sliding into dependency through such self-delusion will make you feel like a stalker the moment they change their minds about having you around. Focusing on their flaws for a while can help offset such over-attachment.

Idealisation is a form of escape from life and from our own self-development. Rather than coping with reality, we create a fantasy in which we can lose ourselves. It's easy to become addicted to a fantasy but it's inevitably disappointing19. Anyone we worship in our imagination can be boring, annoying or even quite obnoxious in reality.

A classic sign that you may have idealised someone is the tendency to disregard counter-evidence that contradicts your wishful sense of who you imagine they are. Your wonderful impression of them may be largely illusory and then you would end up saying "I fell in love with an idea of what they might be like".

Another danger of such obsession is that you may end up devaluing everything else in your life, leaving you with a sense of things being somewhat stale or pointless. It's worth consciously elevating the importance of various things in order not to lose perspective on what you would normally value especially when it comes to progress.

It may become difficult to focus on things that are far less exciting than what our minds have persuaded us we need. But the art of concentrating on something less instantly gratifying and being willing to slowly "get into it" with an open mind can be viewed as an important life skill which is essential to beating any form of addiction.

23. Reassess your excuses for idealising someone

Your mind is likely to come up with interesting reasons why a person would be great for you. A common excuse relates to our simple way of equating different things by similarity or association. For example, there may be something about the person which reminds you of an ex-partner or someone else who was once good for you.

Perhaps they have the same first name or quirky characteristic as someone you used to know. Maybe they fit into a broad category in which you have placed too much faith, such as having the "right" star sign or Myers Briggs personality type. Or maybe it seems that they could never be bad because they work for a charity or hospital.

Broad categories are never enough to tell you what you need to know about a person. And the same goes for anything which you may have in common. It's great if you like the same music and movies or share similar views about politics and religion but that doesn't automatically mean that you have found a great friend or partner in life.

An even bigger risk is the generalisation of a person's good qualities. You may tell yourself that they are "so kind", "so lovely", "so good" and so on just because they have been rather charming up to that point. That doesn't mean that they could never behave like a complete "A-hole" and so it's often a good idea to reserve judgement.

It's precisely that sense of charm, romance or beauty which causes us to get carried away with far-fetched conclusions. What seems like a fateful meeting of destiny driven by irresistible chemistry and an aligning of the planets could easily turn out to be a meaningless, random event of no real significance or consequence.

Wishful thinking can not only make you idealise another person but also cause you to misinterpret something they do as a clear sign of interest in you. Even if you normally consider yourself to be an expert mind-reader, it's worth remembering that romantic thinking involves a somewhat worryingly naive tendency to see the bright side.

24. Be careful about what you worship

When you're dependent, there is also danger of giving too much importance and imagined value to things as well as people. By "things", I am referring not only to real events and physical objects but also to attitudes, principles and ideas. Giving anything too much value and attention could be a consequence of not giving yourself enough.

If we are not willing to love ourselves then we have to find something else to love. When there is not much love on the inside, many people look to the outside world and give external things too much importance. Others find themselves entranced by something which they discover in their inner world, such as a particular belief or notion.

In other words, we are often are willing to see extraordinary potential, beauty, importance or value in something other than ourselves. The danger is that we overdo it and start to worship what then becomes a false idol. What we worship may be good in some ways but we can still overdo our appreciation to the point of unhealthy fixation.

This explains why some dependent people become so intense about things that other people might consider trivial. It's often because they are ready to see anything that is good for them as the answer to all their prayers rather than merely something neat to be added to the general mix of things that contribute to their well-being.

It may also explain why some people get so carried away about whatever principles they consider to be important. Of course, it's good to believe in something but if you are willing to go completely nuts over an issue then there is a good chance that the degree of importance you have given it is partly a symptom of your own suffering.

Overvaluing things is an understandable response to the sense of desperation which many dependent people feel as a result of their own self-neglect. When you feel as though your general happiness level is a 3 out of 10 then anything which offers you the prospect of raising that to a 6 or a 7 may seem like a gift from Heaven itself.

But it's still important to be careful about what you worship rather than merely value. Idolising something automatically lowers you in relation to it, turning you into an overly eager and submissive slave, minion or disciple. You become a wretchedly fixated and unhealthily addicted fanatic willing to do anything for another hit.

25. View what you idealize as a sign of what you could do for yourself

The ideas we fall in love with are still useful when viewed as an expression of our valid needs. Apart from anything else, there could be a valid need to fantasize. After all, exploring your rich imagination can be a very healthy distraction from frustration and boredom so long as you remember never to confuse what you imagine with reality.

But it's also possible to recognize more specific needs in the clues that idealisation produces. For example, you may fantasies about someone acknowledging, connecting with and loving your inner child. That is something that you can start doing for yourself by increasingly noticing and sincerely appreciating your own adorable innocence.

It's not a coincidence when people who do not take proper care of themselves fantasize about someone else behaving like a "caregiver" towards them. Many of those who don't spend enough time listening to their own frustrations, feelings and thoughts will fantasise about someone giving them all of that much-needed attention.

The fantasy of either being saved by someone or of wanting to save someone also points to a valid underlying need. Maybe it's time to become your own savior. A good way to save yourself is to start figuring out what you might realistically do to improve your situation and then taking steps towards making that a reality.

CHAPTER 7

DEPENDENT PERSONALITY DISORDER

Dependent personality disorder (DPD) is one of the most frequently diagnosed personality disorders. It occurs equally in men and women, usually becoming apparent in young adulthood or later as important adult relationships form.

What Are the Symptoms of DPD?

People with DPD become emotionally overdependent on other people and spend great effort trying to please others. People with DPD tend to display needy, passive, and clinging behavior, and have a fear of separation. Other common characteristics of this personality disorder include:

- Inability to make decisions, even everyday decisions like what to wear, without the advice and reassurance of others

- Avoidance of adult responsibilities by acting passive and helpless; dependence on a spouse or friend to make decisions like where to work and live

- Intense fear of abandonment and a sense of devastation or helplessness when relationships end; a person with DPD often moves right into another relationship when one ends.

- Oversensitivity to criticism

- Pessimism and lack of self-confidence, including a belief that they are unable to care for themselves

- Avoidance of disagreeing with others for fear of losing support or approval

- Inability to start projects or tasks because of a lack of self-confidence

- Difficulty being alone

- Willingness to tolerate mistreatment and abuse from others

- Placing the needs of their caregivers above their own

- Tendency to be naive and to fantasize

What Causes DPD?

Although the exact cause of DPD is not known, it most likely involves a combination of biological, developmental, temperamental, and psychological factors. Some researchers believe an authoritarian or overprotective parenting style can lead to the development of dependent personality traits in people who are susceptible to the disorder.

How Is DPD Diagnosed?

A diagnosis of DPD must be distinguished from borderline personality disorder, as the two share common symptoms. In borderline personality disorder, the person responds to fears of abandonment with feelings of rage and emptiness. With DPD, the person responds to the fear with submissiveness and seeks another relationship to maintain his or her dependency.

If most or all the (above) symptoms of DPD are present, the doctor will begin an evaluation by taking a thorough medical and psychiatric history and possibly a basic physical exam. Although there are no laboratory tests to specifically diagnose personality disorders, the doctor might use various diagnostic tests to rule out physical illness as the cause of the symptoms.

If the doctor finds no physical reason for the symptoms, he or she might refer the person to a psychiatrist, psychologist, or other health care professional trained to diagnose and treat mental illnesses. Psychiatrists and psychologists use specially designed interview and assessment tools to evaluate a person for a personality disorder.

How Is DPD Treated?

As is the case with many personality disorders, people with DPD generally do not seek treatment for the disorder itself. Rather, they might seek treatment when a problem in their lives -- often resulting from thinking or behavior related to the disorder -- becomes overwhelming, and they are no longer able to cope. People with DPD are prone to developing depression or anxiety, symptoms that might prompt the individual to seek help.

Psychotherapy (a type of counseling) is the main method of treatment for DPD. The goal of therapy is to help the person with DPD become more active and independent, and to learn to form healthy relationships. Short-term therapy with specific goals is preferred when the focus is on managing behaviors that interfere with functioning. It is often useful for the therapist and patient together to pay attention to the role of therapist in order to recognize and address ways in which the patient may form the same kind of passive reliance in the treatment relationship that happens outside of treatment. Specific strategies might include assertiveness training to help the person with DPD develop self-confidence and cognitive-behavioral therapy (CBT) to help someone develop new attitudes and perspectives about themselves relative to other people and experiences. More meaningful change in someone's personality structure usually is pursued through long-term psychoanalytic or psychodynamic psychotherapy, where early developmental experiences are examined as they may shape the formation of defense mechanisms, coping styles, and patterns of attachment and intimacy in close relationships.

Medication might be used to treat people with DPD who also suffer from related problems such as depression or anxiety. However, medication therapy in itself does not usually treat the core problems caused by personality disorders. In addition, medications should be carefully monitored, because people with DPD could use them inappropriately or abuse certain prescription drugs.

What Are the Complications of DPD?

People with DPD are at risk for depression, anxiety disorders, and phobias, as well as substance abuse. They are also at risk for being abused because they may find themselves willing to do virtually anything to maintain the relationship with a dominant partner or person of authority.

What Is the Outlook for People With DPD?

With psychotherapy (counseling), many people with DPD can learn how to make more independent choices in their lives.

Can DPD Be Prevented?

Although prevention of the disorder might not be possible, treatment of DPD can sometimes allow a person who is prone to this disorder to learn more productive ways of dealing with situations.

The development of personality structure is a complex process that begins from an early age. Psychotherapy aimed at modifying personality may be more successful when begun early, when the patient is highly motivated for change, and when there is a strong working relationship between the therapist and patient.

CONCLUSION

Emotional dependency evolves in an insidious way. Life presents us with many different challenges, and how we feel about ourselves and our ability to cope in large measure determines how we'll meet those challenges. If we're riddled with doubts about our ability to handle things successfully we might not even try, and when we fail to assert ourselves or throw in the towel too quickly or easily, we deny ourselves the opportunity for occasional success. A vicious cycle can then develop: every time we back down, give up, or give in, we only reinforce the notion that we simply can't accomplish our goals. Thinking that way only further impairs our already poor self-image. And that's precisely how emotional dependency develops. Having an impaired sense of both self-efficacy and self-worth can easily predispose a person to seek reassurance, approval and support from others whom they view as stronger, more capable, and more confident. All too often, those with these characteristics are among the overly independent individuals I described earlier. That's how abuse and exploitation can enter a relationship.

Made in the USA
Las Vegas, NV
16 May 2021

23162739R00066